When God Opens The Door

How Ordinary Believers Can Share Jesus
Across the World or Across the Table

Debra Tunney

7710-T Cherry Park Dr, Ste 224
Houston, TX 77095
www.WorldwidePublishingGroup.com

ISBN: 979-8-9995694-0-0

Dedication

I dedicate this book to my husband, Doug Tunney, the best
fisher of men that I know!

Follow me, and I will make you fishers of men. **(Matthew 4:19, KJV)**

Acknowledgments

My heartfelt "Thank you" to every person who has been part of this journey, thank you. Whether you've served beside us, gone on mission with us, or encouraged us from afar, you've helped demonstrate that evangelism is not just for the platform, it's for the sidewalk, the coffee shop, the dinner table, and the nations. May this book reflect the doorways you've already opened, and the lives you've helped lead through them. To God be all the glory.

Contents

Introduction

Dear Reader,

You may be holding this book because you've felt a nudge—a stirring to share your faith, a longing to be used by God, or maybe even a quiet sense that there's more to this life with Him than what you've experienced so far.

I want you to know you are not alone.

This book is for ordinary believers—people like you and me—who have a heart to reach the people who don't yet know Jesus but sometimes wonder how. It's filled with real stories, practical tools, and honest moments from decades of ministry around the world and across the table.

But more than anything, it's an invitation. An invitation to say yes. To walk through the doors God opens. To live a life that echoes in eternity. You don't need to be perfect. You don't need to be eloquent. You just need to be willing.

My prayer is that as you read these pages, the Holy Spirit will whisper to your heart and stir fresh courage. That you'll find your place in God's great rescue mission. And that when He opens the door, you'll walk through—with boldness, love, and joy.

Because someone out there is waiting for the hope you carry.

With love and expectancy,

Debra

Section One
Saying YES to God's Call

Chapter 1
Our Journey of Faith - Messengers to the Nations

The Purpose of This Book

This book is our story—our journey of bringing the Good News to thousands of people. We hope these pages will inspire you to let your light shine in the darkness.

We want to share what we've learned about God's heart for people, which has been our driving force in evangelism. Our goal is to present evangelism in a way that is uplifting and compelling, showing how we can overcome obstacles that hinder our outreach.

Evangelism is not a burden or a duty but a privilege and a joy that flows from God's love. In this book, we share personal stories of how we overcame fears, doubts, and challenges and discovered the beauty and power of being Christ's messengers to the nations.

The world is waiting. Let's go.

So Jesus said to them again, "Peace to you! As the Father has sent Me, I also send you." - John 20:21 (NKJV)

But in your hearts sanctify Christ as Lord. Always be prepared to give a defense to everyone who asks you the reason for the hope that is in you. But respond with gentleness and respect... - 1 Peter 3:15 (BSB)

"Evangelism is not a duty; it is the outflow of a heart transformed by Christ."

Doug's Story

"Doug, tomorrow we are going out on campus to talk to people about Jesus."

I looked Nick straight in the eyes and replied, "No, I don't think I want to do that. I'm not prepared, and I'm busy tomorrow." I was only a few weeks into my newfound faith, and the idea of sharing it with others felt overwhelming. The thought of approaching strangers to talk about Jesus terrified me.

Nick responded, "Doug, part of living for the Lord is having His heart for people and being willing to step out and share that with others."

His words struck a chord. They silenced my excuses and fears. I realized that following Jesus wasn't just about my personal relationship with Him—it was also about telling others.

Evangelism wasn't optional; it was a natural and essential part of my new life in Christ.

The next day, I showed up, still nervous and unprepared. I mostly listened as Nick engaged students in conversation. I silently prayed as he answered their questions.

Some conversations were friendly; some raised deep questions I hadn't even considered. Nick answered what he could, but even he didn't know everything. Yet, I saw how listening and engaging with people opened doors to meaningful discussions about faith.

That experience ignited something in me. I began reading my Bible for hours each day, searching for answers. My prayers shifted from focusing on myself to interceding for others. Over time, I felt God's compassion for those I met, and I developed ways to engage people in meaningful conversations about Jesus and His love.

Since that day in 1972, my life has been driven by a desire to know Him, respond to His heart, and make Him known.

Debra's Story

My dorm room was always filled with girls chatting about their day. We shared our highs and lows, supporting each other through the ups and downs of college life.

One evening, a friend asked, "Debi, what is with this Jesus thing you're into? You talk about God all the time, and we can see it's changing you."

That was my open door.

"I grew up going to church, but when I got to college, I drifted from my faith. Professors challenged my beliefs, and the campus culture pushed me in directions I never intended. I felt lost, searching for something more. My childhood faith wasn't enough to answer the questions I was facing."

The room grew silent. I could tell my friends were listening intently, some even relating to my story.

"It all came to a turning point when I was at the play Hair with a boyfriend who was part of the problem. It wasn't the place where you'd expect a spiritual awakening, but as the music played and I sat beside him, I felt an overwhelming sense of emptiness. I looked at my life, my relationships, and my choices—none of them were leading me anywhere good. In that moment, I thought about Jesus. Amid my confusion, I realized He was the answer I had been searching for."

Taking a deep breath, I continued, "Right there, in that auditorium, I silently prayed. I repented. I surrendered my life to Christ. At that moment, everything changed. The guilt lifted, and my life suddenly had meaning and purpose. I encountered Jesus, and I knew He was real."

That conversation was honest and compelling. One by one, my friends began their own journey of faith. My dorm room became a gathering place for discussions about the Bible and spiritual matters. What started as a simple conversation turned into a small community of believers, growing together in faith.

Talking about Jesus became as natural as breathing. I learned to listen, to understand people's struggles, and to meet them where they were. Jesus is the answer, but first, we must hear the questions people are carrying in their hearts.

Lessons Learned

Evangelism is not about having all the right answers or delivering a flawless presentation. It's about being willing to open our hearts and share our journey with others. People all around us are searching for truth—often silently—and our personal testimony can be the bridge that connects them to faith.

When we step out in obedience, even in our uncertainty, God is faithful to provide the words and the opportunities we need. Sometimes, the most powerful act of evangelism isn't speaking at all. It's listening. By truly hearing others, we show them they matter. And ultimately, it's not just what we say, but the transformation others witness in our lives that speaks the loudest. Our changed lives become a living message of God's grace.

Application

As you think about evangelism, consider the people you interact with daily. Maybe it's a coworker, a classmate, or a neighbor. They may be searching for hope, even if they don't express it outright. Take time to pray for them by name, asking God to open doors for meaningful conversations.

Start by listening. Ask questions that go beyond surface-level interactions. Show genuine interest in their thoughts and struggles. Evangelism isn't about forcing a message but about being present and available when someone is ready to hear.

When the opportunity arises, share your story. It doesn't have to be polished or perfect. Speak from the heart about how Jesus has transformed your life. People connect with authenticity, not rehearsed speeches.

Trust that the Holy Spirit will guide your words and your interactions. Even if you feel unprepared, God can use your willingness to make an impact. The journey of sharing your faith is one of trust, obedience, and love.

Reflection & Discussion Questions

1. What fears or hesitations do you have about sharing your faith? How can you overcome them?

2. How has your own journey of faith prepared you to share Jesus with others?

3. Think of a time when someone's testimony impacted you. What made it compelling?

4. How can you make evangelism a natural part of your daily life?

5. What steps can you take this week to engage in a spiritual conversation with someone?

Chapter 2
Your World View Matters

When I thought how to understand this, it was too painful for me—until I went into the sanctuary of God; then I understood. - Psalm 73:16–17 (NKJV)

That you may become blameless and harmless, children of God without fault in the midst of a crooked and perverse generation, among whom you shine as lights in the world. - Philippians 2:15 (NKJV)

"If you look at the world, you'll be distressed. If you look within, you'll be depressed. If you look at God, you'll be at rest. - Corrie Ten Boom"

"But you tell me over and over and over again, my friend. Ah, you don't believe we're on the eve of destruction." - Barry McGuire, Eve of Destruction

———

It was September 1979. We arrived at Youth With A Mission (YWAM) in Concord, New Hampshire, with our car full of personal belongings, hopes to win the world, and two little girls in tow. We were embarking on a great adventure to bring Jesus to the nations. The world we wanted to reach was in turmoil.

The Three Mile Island nuclear accident sent waves of fear through the nation. Student followers of Ayatollah Khomeini stormed the U.S. embassy in Tehran with sixty-three hostages. Russia invaded Afghanistan.

President Carter articulated the nation's anxiety:

"The threat is nearly invisible in ordinary ways. It is a crisis of confidence... a crisis that strikes at the very heart, soul, and spirit of our national will."

During this, we felt called to be part of the answer. Yet, fear crept in. One day, during a YWAM lecture, a thought gripped me: What about your children?

Before surrendering my life to Jesus, I was certain I didn't want to bring children into a world so broken. Now, that same fear threatened to consume me again.

Until...

God shifted my perspective. He reminded me that He could keep my children. If He had preserved Moses in Pharaoh's court, He could keep my daughters safe in any situation. My job was to remain obedient; the rest was in His hands.

I didn't have to change the whole world—just obey. And in my obedience, lives would be transformed.

Prayer became essential. Through intercession, I learned to focus on God's power, not my concerns. I found rest in knowing He was in control.

Lessons Learned

In a world filled with uncertainty and chaos, it's easy to become overwhelmed by fear. But even amid confusion, God calls us to place our trust in Him. When we embrace a biblical worldview, our perspective shifts—from crisis to Christ—and we begin to see beyond the temporary struggles.

Fear has the power to paralyze, keeping us from stepping into God's purposes, yet obedience unlocks peace and a deeper sense of purpose. What we choose today, in faith or in fear, doesn't just affect us, it shapes the lives of those who come after us. That's why prayer becomes essential. It's through prayer that we lay down our fears, listen to God's voice, and find the strength to walk in His calling with courage and confidence.

Application

Think about the way you view the world. It's easy to be consumed by the chaos, uncertainty, and fear that surrounds us. The news, social media, and personal experiences all shape our perspective. But as followers of Christ, we are called to look beyond the immediate and see with eyes of faith.

Instead of dwelling on what is wrong, choose to focus on what is true. When fear rises, turn to Scripture and prayer. Ask God to help you see circumstances from His perspective rather than your own limited understanding.

Identify areas where fear has held you back. Has it kept you from stepping into a calling? Sharing your faith? Raising children with confidence? Surrender those fears to God and trust that His plans are greater than the world's uncertainties.

God has placed you in this time and place for a reason. Your faith and obedience can make a difference in the lives of those around you. Choose to live boldly, anchored in God's truth, and be a light in the darkness.

Reflection & Discussion Questions

1. How does your worldview influence the way you respond to fear and uncertainty?

2. What are some fears that have held you back from fully embracing God's calling?

3. How can prayer and Scripture help shift your perspective from fear to faith?

4. In what ways can you shine as a light in this dark world?

5. What practical steps can you take to align your worldview with God's truth?

Chapter 3
Dream Job

"For I know the plans I have for you," declares the Lord, "plans to prosper you and not to harm you, plans to give you hope and a future."
- Jeremiah 29:11 (NIV)

"When God closes a door, He opens another—but it's up to us to walk through it."

———

A Divine Appointment

In 1990, Doug received an unexpected invitation to Pastor Ken's office. He had no idea what the purpose of the meeting was.

At the time, Doug was serving as an assistant pastor at Faith Christian Center, one of the largest churches in New Hampshire. His role primarily involved filling in wherever needed, handling tasks that the other four pastors didn't have time for. He worked long hours, from 9 to 5, in a suit and tie, answering phone calls, addressing concerns, and managing day-to-day tasks. Though he was officially in ministry, this role didn't exactly match Doug's passion. It was far from the hands-on ministry he had done before as a youth pastor and a YWAM missionary.

When the church underwent restructuring, his position was eliminated along with several others. Doug felt a sense of relief as he moved on from a job that didn't suit him. Six months later, he found himself back running his commercial cleaning business.

Then, one day, Pastor Ken invited him into his office.

The moment Pastor Ken walked in with a smile, the tension eased, and the room felt warmer. "A lot has happened this year," Pastor Ken began. "The elders and I have seen God's work in your life, and we're grateful you stayed with Faith Christian Center. We've noticed that your business is doing well again, and we really appreciate your servant attitude, helping with various tasks around the church."

Doug, still uncertain about the purpose of the meeting, smiled and replied, "And the reason for this meeting is?"

Pastor Ken leaned in and asked a question Doug didn't expect: "If you could do anything in ministry, what would that be?"

The question caught Doug off guard. There was a long pause before he spoke up.

"I have a heart for evangelism," Doug said slowly, thinking carefully. "Ever since I began walking with Jesus, sharing the Gospel has been a central part of my life. Most believers don't share their faith, but people need to know the Lord. I want to help others overcome what holds them back and equip them to take the message of Jesus to those who don't know Him. Not just our church, but the whole Church in New Hampshire. That would be my dream job."

Pastor Ken didn't say anything at first. Instead, he handed Doug a notepad. "Doug, would you write that down? This could be your new job description if you're open to joining our staff again."

In that moment, Pastor Ken opened a door for Doug into a role that perfectly matched his gifts and passion.

Doug swapped his suit for more casual clothes, excited about reaching Manchester, NH with the Gospel. His days were now dedicated to praying for the city and seeking God's strategy for reaching the people there. The following Sunday, Doug couldn't wait to announce the new outreach.

"Good morning, church! This Saturday, we're going out into the city to share the Gospel, and we want to invite you to join us. We'll meet here at 10 a.m. and spend two hours talking to people and sharing our faith."

Doug's excitement was contagious, and 30 people showed up for the first outreach. They were eager to share Jesus and had the availability to do so. However, the day didn't go as smoothly as Doug had hoped. Parking was a challenge, one of the vans got lost and was 30 minutes late, and people on the streets mostly ignored them. There were even some tense moments, with team members confronting strangers and having disagreements amongst themselves. One or two harsh words were exchanged, like "Do you realize you're going to burn in hell?"

At the end of the day, they gathered back at the church for a debrief.

"I shared the Gospel with a young woman today, and she was so open. She received Jesus, and we prayed together," Jenny shared with the group. However, her positive report was met with lukewarm responses, likely from the exhaustion and frustrations of the day.

Doug tried to stay positive. "The first time out is always the hardest," he said with a smile. "Next Saturday will go better. See you then and bring a friend!"

The following Saturday, only Jenny from the previous week showed up, along with two new faces. That's when Doug realized that better planning and preparation were necessary for their future outreaches. So, before their next session, they spent more time in prayer, seeking God's heart for the mission. Prayer became their foundation, as they trusted God to lead them in reaching the city.

Doug's role as an evangelist became clear. As we read in Ephesians 4:11-12, part of his calling was to equip others for ministry.

And He Himself gave some to be apostles, some prophets, some evangelists, and some pastors and teachers, for the equipping of the saints for the work of ministry, for the edifying of the body of Christ... - Ephesians 4:11-12 (NKJV)

Doug embraced the responsibility of equipping believers for the work of the Gospel. Jesus had given a clear model for ministry: Do, Teach, Send. And that's exactly what Doug set out to do.

Lessons Learned

God often reveals His plans for our lives in the most unexpected moments—interrupting the ordinary with divine direction. When we respond with obedience, those moments turn into opportunities to participate in something far greater than ourselves.

While passion ignites the journey, it's not enough on its own. Preparation and strategy are essential if we're to walk in wisdom and bear lasting fruit. Evangelism, too, is not a one-time act—it demands persistence, a foundation of prayer, and a commitment to equipping others for the mission. At its core, a true calling isn't about self-fulfillment. It's about laying down our lives to serve others and to advance the Kingdom of God in every sphere He sends us.

Application

What has God placed on your heart? Maybe there's a dream or calling you've hesitated to pursue. Like Doug, you may have felt stuck in a role that didn't fit your passion. Take time to pray and ask God what doors He might be opening for you.

If you've stepped out and faced challenges, don't be discouraged. Every great move of God requires persistence. Learn from setbacks, refine your approach, and trust that God is working through you.

Identify ways you can start equipping others. Whether through mentorship, teaching, or simply encouraging someone, you can help others grow in their faith and calling.

Reflection & Discussion Questions

1. Have you ever experienced a season where you felt stuck in a role that didn't align with your passion? How did you handle it?

2. How can you better prepare yourself for the calling God has placed on your heart?

3. What are some practical ways you can share your faith more effectively?

4. How can you encourage and equip others in their walk with Christ?

5. What steps can you take this week to align yourself with God's plan for your life?

Chapter 4
Beautiful Feet

How then shall they call on Him in whom they have not believed? And how shall they believe in Him of whom they have not heard? And how shall they hear without a preacher? And how shall they preach unless they are sent? As it is written: "How beautiful are the feet of those who preach the gospel of peace, who bring glad tidings of good things!" - Romans 10:14–15 (NKJV)

Then He said to His disciples, "The harvest truly is plentiful, but the laborers are few. Therefore, pray the Lord of the harvest to send out laborers into His harvest." - Matthew 9:37–38 (NKJV)

"Out of the seats and into the streets—that's my new motto!" – Outreach Team Member

―――――

A Team Transformed

"For some of you, this was your first outreach. Let's take a few minutes to talk about your experiences and reflections," Doug invited the team.

They gathered in a circle, energized and reflective. Unlike the cold-call outreach a few weeks earlier, this time the team was well-prepared. Doug had answered their questions, trained them to use The Wordless Book tract, coached them in sharing personal testimonies, and guided them through focused prayer before heading out. They didn't have all the answers, but a calm confidence and unity filled the group. They had taken a step of faith.

As team members shared their experiences, the room buzzed with emotion:

"I was surprised by how open people were to talking with me. Hearing helpful comments reminded me how important it is to make connections."

"That wasn't my experience. It felt like everyone was rushing by, and the few who stopped didn't seem open to talking about God. I'm feeling a bit discouraged."

"The young man I spoke to thanked me. He said he'd been praying for God to send someone to tell him the truth."

"I spoke to a grandmother today who was grieving. She'd recently lost her grandson and was heartbroken. All I could do was hug her and pray that God would comfort her."

"Out of the seats and into the streets—that's my new motto! I saw first-hand what I've been missing. The people I spoke to were so kind."

"The training gave me the confidence to start conversations."

"This experience has changed me. I had distanced myself from the people who need Jesus. I thought they were all against us Christians, but most were so open. I prayed with three teenage boys who asked Jesus into their lives."

Doug beamed as he listened. "Today, you had beautiful feet," he said, referencing Romans 10. "Many people heard about Jesus because you took a step of faith."

He went on to explain the common experience of isolation that many believers feel. "Within 18 months of coming to Christ, most new believers lose nearly all their non-Christian friendships. It's not intentional, but it happens. That's why we must be intentional about going to people and sharing Jesus."

He paused. "You've probably heard, 'Preach the Gospel, and if necessary, use words.' It's often attributed to St. Francis of Assisi, but he never said that. The idea is well-meaning, but it's incomplete. We need both the testimony of our lives and the clarity of our words. The Bible makes that clear."

Doug's reminder about FEAR—False Evidence Appearing Real—landed well. "You overcame fear today. You stepped out. And because you did, people heard the Gospel."

Doug also reminded them of Jesus' call to His disciples: "Follow Me, and I will make you fishers of men." Whether or not they had experience fishing, they understood the metaphor—Jesus was inviting them into a mission.

He continued: "The church is called to go into the harvest. That's the commission Jesus gave us. Church buildings are wonderful, but we're not called to wait for people to come to us—we're called to go to them.

Lessons Learned

One of the most important foundations for effective outreach is preparation. When we take time to equip ourselves, it builds confidence and clarity for the task ahead. Surprisingly, people are often more open to spiritual conversations than we imagine.

When we listen well and genuinely care, hearts begin to open, and opportunities emerge. In many cases, sharing the Gospel is met not with resistance, but with sincere gratitude. Fear is a natural response, but it doesn't have to control us. With prayer, practical training, and a willingness to take that first step, fear gives way to faith in action. Evangelism is not just a responsibility—it's a sacred privilege. When we walk in obedience, we become part of God's redemptive work in the lives of others.

Application

Take time to prepare before sharing your faith—study the Gospel, practice your testimony, and pray for boldness. Remember that evangelism is not about being perfect; it's about being willing.

Think about your relationships. Are there people in your life who haven't heard about Jesus? Pray for them by name and ask God for an opportunity to reach out.

Reflect on your fears. What holds you back from sharing your faith? Write those things down and bring them to God. Let Him turn your fear into faith.

Commit to being intentional. Look for opportunities this week to take a step toward someone who needs hope.

Reflection & Discussion Questions

1. What part of the outreach experience encouraged or challenged you the most?

2. How did preparation impact your confidence and effectiveness?

3. What is one fear that often holds you back from sharing your faith?

4. Who in your life needs to hear the Gospel, and how can you reach them?

5. What does it mean for you to have "beautiful feet" in your everyday life?

Chapter 5
Called to Equip

And it was He who gave some to be apostles, some to be prophets, some to be evangelists, and some to be pastors and teachers, to equip the saints for works of ministry, to build up the body of Christ, until we all reach unity in the faith and in the knowledge of the Son of God, as we mature to the full measure of the stature of Christ. - Ephesians 4:11–13 (NIV)

"Evangelism isn't just for the gifted, it's for the obedient. And obedience can be taught, modeled, and multiplied."

———

The School of Evangelism—Equipping Evangelists for the Gospel

As believers, we are all called to share the Gospel and be fishers of men, but among us, God appoints evangelists to not only proclaim the Good News but also to equip others to do the same. The role of an Equipping Evangelist is twofold: to actively engage in evangelism and to train others to confidently and effectively share their faith.

Through countless outreach efforts, it became increasingly evident that people needed more than just an invitation to go—they needed equipping. Thus, the vision for the School of Evangelism and Ministry was born: a program dedicated to reproducing Gospel messengers and discipling new believers.

The Birth of the School

As outreach participation grew, so did the realization that many believers wanted to share their faith but lacked the confidence and clarity to do so. A survey revealed common struggles:

- Fear of rejection
- Not knowing how to start conversations
- Uncertainty about answering hard questions
- Feelings of inadequacy
- The false belief that evangelism is only for the gifted

The School of Evangelism was created in response. We structured it to include both biblical teaching and hands-on practice, giving believers a place to learn, grow, and step into their calling.

The Mission: Do, Then Teach

We followed Jesus' example—He did, then He taught. Our team committed to being active evangelists, and from our real-life experiences, we developed practical lessons and strategies to pass on. Equipping others wasn't optional. It was essential!

The Structure of the School

The School of Evangelism's curriculum included:

- Understanding the Gospel Message
- What is the Gospel?
- Why is it Good News?
- How to clearly present the message of salvation
- Overcoming Fear and Obstacles
- Identifying and dismantling common fears
- Handling rejection with grace
- Relying on the Holy Spirit for courage and wisdom
- Developing Evangelistic Strategies
- Different approaches: conversational, testimonial, direct
- Engaging with various audiences
- Turning everyday interactions into Gospel opportunities

- Apologetics and Defending the Faith
- Responding to tough questions with grace and truth
- Understanding worldviews
- Showing the relevance of Scripture
- Hands-On Training
- Engaging in real outreach: streets, homes, and one-on-one
- Partnering with experienced evangelists for mentorship

Lessons Learned

Sharing our faith isn't reserved for a select few—it's something every believer can learn to do. With the right training and intentional practice, confidence grows, and what once felt intimidating becomes second nature.

Evangelism starts to feel less like a duty and more like a natural outflow of a life fully surrendered to God. But the calling doesn't stop with us. When we take time to equip others, our impact is multiplied far beyond what we could ever accomplish alone. The role of an evangelist isn't just to go—it's to lead, to train, and to send others into the harvest field, empowered to do the same.

Application

Are you willing to be equipped? Evangelism is not reserved for the fearless or the eloquent—it is for the faithful.

Consider how you might benefit from structured training. Are there people in your life you long to reach but feel unsure how? The answer may lie in equipping.

And if you've been equipped, consider this: Who can you now equip? Just as you've learned, so you can teach. Just as you've been sent, so you can send.

Take time to reflect on your own readiness and commitment. The harvest is still plentiful. The laborers are still few.

Reflection & Discussion Questions

1. What fears or misconceptions have kept you from sharing your faith?

2. How might a training program like the School of Evangelism help you grow?

3. Have you ever helped equip someone else to share the Gospel? What did you learn?

4. What step can you take this week to become more confident in evangelism?

5. Who around you could benefit from being mentored in evangelism?

Chapter 6
Evangelism Focus

"Follow Me, and I will make you fishers of men." - Mark 1:17 (NKJV)

"Go into all the world and preach the gospel to all creation. He who has believed and has been baptized shall be saved; but he who has disbelieved shall be condemned." - Mark 16:15-16 (NASB)

"Evangelism is not a job for a few specialists. It's the joyful response of anyone who has met the Savior."

———

I remember the first time I realized that evangelism wasn't just for pastors or missionaries—it was for me. A neighbor had gone through a personal crisis, and I felt the Holy Spirit prompt me to share a word of encouragement. I hesitated, unsure of what to say, but I simply offered to pray with her.

That small moment of obedience opened the door to a conversation about Jesus. She said, "No one's ever talked to me about God like this." That day, I learned that evangelism is less about perfect words and more about showing up when God opens the door.

God's Heart for the World

From Genesis to Revelation, we see God's desire to reconcile people to Himself. The first command to "Go and be a blessing" (Genesis 12:2–3) sets the tone for God's missional heart. Jesus reinforced this when He called His followers to be fishers of men (Mark 1:17).

Jesus Calls Believers

Jesus gave both a first and a final command:

First Command – *"Follow Me, and I will make you fishers of men."* - Mark 1:17 (NKJV)

Last Command – *"Go into all the world and preach the gospel..."* - Mark 16:15–16 (NKJV)

His last words on earth carried weight – *"You will receive power when the Holy Spirit comes on you, and you will be My witnesses..."* - Acts 1:8–9 (NIV)

Did the Early Church Obey?

Not at first. Acts 8:1 shows us that persecution had to scatter them before they went. Sometimes we wait until things get uncomfortable before we obey God's call to reach out. But even then, God uses all things to spread His Word.

Obedience Brings Blessing

As you go, God goes to those you care most about. When we step out to share the gospel, God prepares hearts. He blesses our obedience, multiplies our efforts, and meets people through our words and presence.

Lessons Learned

Evangelism isn't just a job title or a role for a few—it's a way of life for every believer. According to 2 Corinthians 5:18–20, we have all been given **the ministry of reconciliation** and are called to be **ambassadors for Christ**, representing Him in our everyday lives. This calling doesn't require a microphone or a stage. It simply requires a heart that's willing to say "yes" to God and a readiness to share His love wherever He leads. When we embrace this identity, evangelism becomes less about position and more about presence—being available to reflect Jesus in every conversation, every interaction, and every opportunity.

Application

Ask God today - "Who in my life needs to know You?"

"How can I reflect Your heart for the world?"

Start where you are. Open your heart. And when He opens the door—walk through it.

Reflection & Discussion Questions

1. What does it mean to you personally to be a "fisher of men"?

2. Why do you think Jesus made His last command a commission to go?

3. Have you ever hesitated to share your faith? What held you back?

4. How can you grow in obedience to God's call to be His ambassador?

5. Who has God placed on your heart to reach with the gospel?

———

Saying YES to God's Call

There's something powerful about a simple "yes" to God. It doesn't have to be polished or perfect—it just has to be sincere. This section begins with the heart of our journey: the moment we said yes.

When we respond to God's call with willingness, He takes our ordinary lives and writes an extraordinary story. These chapters are filled with the early steps of faith, the unexpected turns, and the quiet nudges that led us into a life of evangelism and mission. Wherever you are in your journey, our prayer is that these stories stir a fresh courage in you—to say yes to whatever door God is opening next.

Section Two
Messengers

Chapter 7
Ambassadors – Representing the Kingdom of God

All this is from God, who reconciled us to himself through Christ and gave us the ministry of reconciliation: that God was reconciling the world to himself in Christ, not counting people's sins against them. And he has committed to us the message of reconciliation. We are therefore Christ's ambassadors, as though God were making his appeal through us. We implore you on Christ's behalf: Be reconciled to God. – 2 Corinthians 5:18–20 (NIV)

For I am not ashamed of the gospel, for it is the power of God for salvation to everyone who believes. – Romans 1:16 (NASB)

"You are not just a messenger. You are a representative of the King."

––––––

Ambassadors don't speak on their own authority. They reflect the will and the heart of the one who sent them. Let your life reflect the glory of your King.

Liberia and the Weight of Representation

In the early 1990s, Liberia was enduring a devastating war. Our church, Faith Christian Center, sent a team with a container full of millions of dollars in relief supplies. This act of compassion opened a door for us to be invited to a reception hosted by the President of Liberia and attended by the U.S. ambassador.

The event was beautiful. Gold-trimmed plates, fresh flowers, formal greetings—the works. When the ambassador entered the room, the atmosphere shifted. "Hail to the Chief" played. People stood in respect. This man represented a nation.

In that moment, the Lord whispered to my heart: "You are My ambassador. This man represents a country, but you represent My Kingdom. I have sent you to represent Me."

That thought changed me. I realized that I was called to be holy because I represent the Holy One. I began to consider how my actions—even small ones—reflected on my King. Public outbursts, hidden compromises, careless words—they no longer just affected me. They affected how people saw Jesus.

To be Christ's ambassador is the highest calling. It requires humility, authenticity, and surrender.

Lessons Learned

As ambassadors for Christ, we go not in our own strength, but with the authority of the One who sends us. We represent God—not ourselves—and carry His message, not our personal opinions. The Gospel is His truth, and we are simply the messengers. Our responsibility is obedience, not results. It is God alone who produces the fruit from the seeds we plant. That's why prayer is essential. Through prayer, we stay aligned with the heart of the One we represent, walking in step with His Spirit. And integrity must remain at the core of our witness, because the way we live either reinforces or undermines the message we proclaim.

Application

Understand that you are an ambassador for Christ. This means more than just sharing a message—it means embodying it. Build open, trusting relationships with those who don't yet know Jesus. Let them see your process of being transformed.

Don't hide your struggles. God is not afraid to show His work in progress. People don't need perfect Christians; they need real ones.

Represent your King in word and in action. Let your life be a testimony of reconciliation.

Reflection & Discussion Questions

1. What does it mean to you to be an ambassador for Christ?

2. How does your life reflect the King you represent?

3. What areas might need to come into alignment with your calling?

4. How can you live more transparently before those who are watching your life?

5. Who around you needs to see Jesus in action through you?

Chapter 8
Get Equipped

But in your hearts revere Christ as Lord. Always be prepared to give an answer to everyone who asks you to give the reason for the hope that you have. But do this with gentleness and respect. – 1 Peter 3:15 (NIV)

He answered, "Whether he is a sinner or not, I do not know. One thing I do know: I was blind but now I see!" – John 9:25 (NIV)

"You may not know everything, but your story is something no one can deny."

———

You may not have all the answers, but you have the Answer—Jesus. Start where you are, share what you know, and let God use your story.

Learning to Share with What You Know

I remember the early days of my Christian walk. I was a college student with a new faith and a burning desire to share Jesus with my friends. The only problem? I didn't know much. I hadn't studied theology or learned apologetics. But I did know this: I had surrendered my life to the Lord, repented of my sins, and trusted Him with my future. That was my story.

Like the man in John 9, I couldn't explain everything, but I could say: "One thing I know—I was blind, and now I see." That simple, honest testimony touched lives. I didn't need all the answers—I needed to share what I knew. And that became the foundation for everything I would later learn.

I heard lots of questions in those days. Some I couldn't answer. But instead of letting that stop me, I committed to becoming a learner. The more I searched for answers, the more my faith grew. I discovered that getting equipped wasn't about mastering every argument—it was about being faithful with what God had done in my life and continuing to grow.

Lessons Learned

You don't need to have all the answers before you begin sharing your faith. What you do have—your personal story—is powerful and deeply relatable. While apologetics can be a helpful tool in addressing tough questions, it's often love, honesty, and humility that open hearts to the Gospel.

Embracing the posture of a learner builds both confidence and understanding, allowing you to grow as you go. The good news is that God isn't looking for perfection—He's looking for willingness. When we step out in faith, He equips us with what we need, moment by moment.

Application

Take time to write out your story—your testimony. What was your life like before Christ? How did you encounter Him? What has changed?

Commit to becoming a lifelong learner. Find a resource—whether a book, podcast, or Bible study—that helps you better understand your faith.

Don't be afraid to say, "I don't know, but I'll find out." It shows humility and sincerity.

Keep sharing, even if you feel unprepared. God will meet you in the moment and give you the words you need.

Reflection & Discussion Questions

1. What part of your testimony could be encouraging to someone else?

2. What's one fear you have about not knowing what to say?

3. How can you begin equipping yourself today to grow more confident?

4. Who could you share your story with this week?

5. What resources have helped you grow in your ability to share the Gospel?

Chapter 9
Overcoming the Obstacles

At the same time, pray also for us, that God may open to us a door for the word, to declare the mystery of Christ, on account of which I am in prison, that I may make it clear, which is how I ought to speak. - Colossians 4:3-4 (ESV)

"To do and then to teach—this is the path of an equipping evangelist."

————

A Call to Equip Through the School of Evangelism

These times of outreach were so fulfilling. Each week, new people would join and many people were reached with the Gospel. As our team continued to grow, we realized that to be more effective, we needed a class where we could impart all the insights we were learning on the streets. This led to the vision of creating a School of Evangelism and Ministry—a program that would help us reproduce messengers of the Gospel and provide a structure to disciple new believers.

We knew that all believers are called to share the Gospel, to be fishers of men. But we also began to see that some of us were called as evangelists—not only to share the message ourselves, but to equip others to do the work of ministry and build up the church. We were being called as equipping evangelists.

Our model became simple and clear: **Do, then Teach**. We would lead by example, share from real-life experience, and empower others through training and practical opportunities to share their faith.

35

The first step in developing the School of Evangelism was a survey. We asked participants about their past experience sharing their faith and what led them to join the class. We also asked them what obstacles had held them back.

Their responses shaped our curriculum and approach. We designed the course to address their fears and needs—making it a place where real growth could happen. And just like that, the School of Evangelism was born.

Lessons Learned

Ministry becomes most effective when we lead by example, showing others what it looks like to live out the Gospel in everyday life. When we take time to equip and empower others, the impact of the message is multiplied far beyond what we could accomplish alone. Structured training helps break through fear, replacing hesitation with confidence and clarity.

Every believer has a role to play in fulfilling the Great Commission—no one is exempt. Evangelists are not only called to go themselves, but to raise up others and send them into the harvest field, fully equipped to share Christ wherever they are sent.

Application

If you've been growing in your ability to share the Gospel, consider how you might help others do the same. Who can you train? Who can you walk with?

Think about the barriers that once held you back. How did you overcome them? Those experiences can become stepping-stones for someone else.

Start small. Invite someone to join you in outreach. Share what you've learned. Ask questions and listen to their fears.

Remember: the role of the equipping-evangelist is not to impress others with knowledge, but to empower them with faith and practice.

Reflection & Discussion Questions

1. What insight from your own outreach experience could help someone else?

2. How might God be calling you to equip others?

3. What obstacles do you see others facing when it comes to evangelism?

4. How can you create a supportive environment where people can learn and grow?

5. What is one step you can take this week to start equipping others for the work of evangelism?

Chapter 10
Rebuilding Connections – Overcoming the SDI Syndrome

The Word became flesh and blood and moved into the neighborhood. We saw the glory with our own eyes, the one-of-a-kind glory, like Father, like Son, generous inside and out, true from start to finish. - John 1:14 (MSG)

"We are not saved to be isolated. We are saved to be sent."

———

As Christians, our goal is to reach people with the Gospel of Jesus Christ. However, often, we find ourselves struggling with what we call the SDI syndrome: Saved, Delivered, and Isolated.

After we begin our walk with the Lord, something subtle and unintended happens—we lose touch with the world around us.

In our pursuit of holy living, we often retreat into Christian bubbles, disconnecting from the very people we're called to reach. Our friendships change, our social circles shift, and before long, we find ourselves surrounded only by other believers.

The mission of Jesus is not just about personal transformation but also about proclaiming that transformation to others. Most people come to faith not through sermons or crusades, but through relationships— through family, friends, neighbors, and coworkers. That's why we must be intentional about rebuilding those connections outside the church walls.

Our culture often views Christians as legalistic, hypocritical, and out of touch. But that image doesn't reflect who we really are. We are people marked by love, compassion, and a desire to see others come to know the grace of Jesus. But to change this perception, we must go where people are—into the neighborhoods, workplaces, and community spaces—just like Jesus did.

Jesus' invitation to His disciples was clear: *Follow Me, and I will make you fishers of men*. And His command was equally clear: *Go into all the world and preach the Gospel*. Yet church culture often becomes inward-focused. We need to realign ourselves with Christ's outward mission.

One practical way we've done this is through **Prayer Stations**. With a simple question—"May I pray for you?"—walls begin to come down. It opens the door for real connection. It shows compassion. It makes room for the Gospel to be shared naturally, without pressure.

Still, many believers hesitate. Fear, apathy, feelings of inadequacy, or guilt over personal struggles keep them from stepping out. But if we wait until we feel worthy or fully prepared, we may never go. We must remember: our calling is not about our perfection, but about Christ's power in us.

The Gospel can't stay behind the walls of the church. It must move into the neighborhood.

Lessons Learned

Isolation often happens slowly, without us even noticing. But it can be reversed when we intentionally reach out to others with the love of Christ. Evangelism is most impactful when it happens through relationships and real-life connections, not just events or presentations. To truly reach people, our lives must move beyond Christian circles and into the everyday spaces where others live, work, and struggle.

Practical tools—like **Prayer Stations**—can help break down fear and open natural doors for Gospel conversations. The good news is, we don't have to be perfect to be effective. We simply need to be willing, available, and obedient to God's leading.

Application

Take inventory of your current relationships. How many of your regular interactions are with people who don't yet know Jesus? Ask God to highlight people in your life who need connection and compassion.

Break out of the comfort zone. Go where people are. Get involved in your community, attend events, and be present in everyday spaces with Gospel intentionality.

Use simple tools like offering prayer or asking questions that show genuine care. Let your presence be marked by love, not judgment.

And most importantly, remember that Jesus already moved into the neighborhood—He's inviting you to do the same.

Reflection & Discussion Questions

1. Have you experienced the SDI syndrome in your walk with Christ? What led to it?

2. What are some practical ways you can rebuild connections with non-believers?

3. Why do you think people are more open to the Gospel through relationships than other means?

4. What are some barriers that hold you back from going out? How can you overcome them?

5. How can your church create space for reconnecting with the community?

Chapter 11
Conquering Fear

For God has not given us a spirit of fear, but of power and of love and of a sound mind. – 2 Timothy 1:7 (NKJV)

There is no fear in love. But perfect love drives out fear, because fear has to do with punishment. The one who fears is not made perfect in love. – 1 John 4:18 (NIV)

"The very things that have made people lost have made them ready." - Ron Hutchcraft

Conquering Fear in Evangelism

Many Christians long to share the life-transforming message of the Gospel yet fear often holds them back. Fear whispers doubts: "You're not ready," "They don't want to hear it," "You'll mess it up." As a result, even those passionate about Christ often remain on the sidelines.

But the world is filled with people carrying deep questions, pain, and spiritual hunger. The key to overcoming fear in evangelism is to identify the barriers and replace them with truth.

The Fear of Rejection

Most of us dread being dismissed or ridiculed. Yet Jesus was rejected. Paul was rejected. They kept going, not because rejection disappeared, but because the mission mattered more. We are not responsible for the outcome—only our obedience. When we shift our focus from ourselves to God's calling, fear loses its grip.

The Fear of Being Judgmental

In a world that prizes tolerance, we may fear being perceived as condemning. But true evangelism isn't about judgment—it's about love. When we engage with humility and respect, people see our sincerity. Jesus met people where they were; we're called to do the same.

The Fear of Offending Others

Faith is deeply personal. We fear pushing people away. But the Gospel, shared in love, brings healing. It's not our job to avoid all discomfort—it's to speak the truth in love and let God do the rest.

The Fear of Closed Doors

Some worry that no one will listen. But God opens hearts. Even when doors seem closed, we can pray, build relationships, and trust that God is working. Our faithfulness today may lead to fruit tomorrow.

The Fear of Embarrassment

We fear stumbling over our words or not having answers. But God doesn't call us to be flawless—just faithful. The Holy Spirit gives us what we need. It's okay not to have all the answers. What matters is stepping out.

The Fear of Being Labeled

Christians today are often mischaracterized. We fear being seen as hypocrites or bigots. But evangelism is not about proving our perfection—it's about pointing to Jesus. Authenticity, humility, and love disarm suspicion and will open hearts to hear the Gospel.

Lessons Learned

Fear has a way of distorting reality, making challenges seem bigger and more threatening than they truly are—and too often, it silences our witness. But when we understand that rejection is not personal, but spiritual, it frees us to keep sharing the Gospel with boldness.

God never asks us to go in our own strength; He equips and empowers those who are willing to step out in faith. And while we may expect resistance, many people are more open than we imagine—especially when approached with genuine respect and compassion. Ultimately, our motivation must be rooted in love, not fear. It is love that compels us, sustains us, and makes our message truly compelling.

Application

Evaluate what fears have been holding you back. Name them, write them down, and surrender them to God. Ask for His strength and boldness.

Look for opportunities to start small. Offer prayer, share part of your testimony, or ask a spiritual question. Trust the Holy Spirit to guide you.

Meditate on God's promises. He hasn't given you fear—He's given you power, love, and self-control.

Remind yourself: You are not ashamed of the Gospel—it is the power of God for salvation.

Reflection & Discussion Questions

1. What fear most often keeps you from sharing your faith?

2. Can you recall a time when fear held you back from speaking up? What would you do differently now?

3. What truth from God's Word helps you overcome fear?

4. How can love for others become a stronger motivator than fear of rejection?

5. What's one step of courage you can take this week to share the Gospel?

Chapter 12
Come Clean

The goal of this command is love, which comes from a pure heart and a good conscience and a sincere faith. – 1 Timothy 1:5 (NIV)

Holding faith, and a good conscience; which some having put away concerning faith have made shipwreck. – 1 Timothy 1:19 (KJV)

"Everybody's got a story, and it's not the one they're telling." - Donald Miller

———

God hasn't called you to be flawless—He's called you to be faithful. Come clean, be bold, and share the hope you've found.

Living a Life of Faith with a Pure Heart

Honesty and transparency have lost out to image and performance. In a world that celebrates outward success and filters every flaw, it's easy—even in the church—to adopt a public persona that hides the compromised places in our lives. We want to be accepted, respected, and admired, but beneath the surface, we know when things aren't right.

Often, we live in quiet compromise, justifying choices that distance us from God's best. We may tell ourselves, "I'm okay, you're okay," and go about life hoping no one notices. But we know. We feel the weight of guilt. And nothing magnifies that weight more than stepping into a place of ministry.

When you begin to respond to God's call to share the Gospel and take steps of faith, that underlying guilt rises quickly:

- "How can you talk to others when you are so..."
- "You're a hypocrite."
- "If people knew your past, you'd have nothing to say."

This fear of exposure is paralyzing. The label "hypocrite" is a weapon of shame that silences us. 1 Timothy 1:19 warns us that if we put away faith and a good conscience, we risk shipwrecking our lives. And sadly, many do. Rather than push through and pursue healing and freedom, we shrink back. We disqualify ourselves.

But God's invitation is not to shame—it's to transformation.

When we bring our compromised areas to Jesus, He doesn't push us away. He restores us. He purifies our hearts and renews our confidence so we can walk boldly in His calling. God doesn't wait for perfection—He asks for repentance. And when we walk with a clean heart, we walk with boldness.

You don't have to fake it. You don't have to be perfect. But you do need to be honest—with God and with yourself. And as you surrender the hidden places, you'll discover new courage to live and share the Gospel authentically.

Lessons Learned

A compromised life leads to internal conflict, making it difficult to speak with clarity or conviction about the Gospel. When we fear being exposed, we often hesitate to step out in faith, holding back what God is calling us to share. But the Lord isn't looking for perfection—He's looking for honesty and repentance.

When we live from a pure heart, we begin to walk in a new boldness and confidence that comes not from ourselves, but from Him. Our qualification doesn't come from our performance or record; it comes from the unshakable grace of Christ, who calls and empowers us to be His witnesses.

Application

Examine your heart. Are there areas of compromise that have been tripping you up? Bring them into the light. Talk to God honestly. Confess what's weighing on you, and receive His forgiveness.

Ask Him to give you a clean heart and renew a right spirit within you. This is where real freedom begins.

Take a step today. Don't wait to feel worthy—trust that Jesus makes you worthy. Share your story, flaws and all. Let people see the grace of God in your life.

When your heart is pure, your voice is strong. And the world needs to hear your voice.

Reflection & Discussion Questions

1. What areas of compromise have silenced your voice in sharing the Gospel?

2. How does fear of being labeled a hypocrite impact your willingness to witness?

3. Why do you think God values honesty and repentance more than perfection?

4. What does it mean to live with a clean heart and a sincere faith?

5. What step can you take this week to surrender compromised areas to God?

Chapter 13
Apathy

Each of you should use whatever gift you have received to serve others, as faithful stewards of God's grace in its various forms. – 1 Peter 4:10 (NIV)

Everyone who calls on the name of the Lord will be saved. How, then, can they call on the one they have not believed in? And how can they believe in the one of whom they have not heard? And how can they hear without someone preaching to them? And how can they preach unless they are sent? As it is written: "How beautiful are the feet of those who bring good news!" – Romans 10:13–15 (NIV)

He is patient with you, not wanting anyone to perish, but everyone to come to repentance. – 2 Peter 3:9 (NIV)

"The Gospel isn't about winning arguments—it's about winning hearts."

––––––

Reengaging starts with remembering: the Gospel is about relationship. Let love lead you back into the mission.

Apathy doesn't shout—it whispers. It creeps in quietly, masked as busyness, distraction, or even theological complexity. It says, "Someone else will do it." Or worse, "It doesn't really need to be done."

It's the older brother in the prodigal son story, near the Father but not understanding His heart. It's the disconnect that comes from too much technology and not enough community. We scroll, but don't see. We text, but don't talk. We walk by, but don't notice.

We've traded front porch conversations for echo chambers. And somewhere along the way, we've stopped seeing people as sons and daughters and started seeing them as strangers—or worse, as "the lost."

But God doesn't see strangers. He sees names. Faces. Stories. Sons and daughters waiting to be welcomed home.

We need a second touch—like the blind man in Mark's Gospel who first saw people as trees walking. Only after the second touch did he see them clearly. We need God to help us see people not as projects, but as individuals loved by Him. Evangelism isn't about collecting "scalps" or hitting quotas. It's about welcoming family home.

The Gospel is relational. We are not inviting people to a club—they are being invited into a family. And our job is not to argue them in, but to love them in. Gunshot weddings never last; neither do conversions born from pressure. Love, not force, is the bridge to truth.

We live in a society starving for connection. Books on evangelism from decades ago often no longer fit our culture. We don't need formulas—we need friendships. Real conversations. Real love. Real prayer. That's what people are longing for. And it starts with us.

Lessons Learned

Apathy creates distance—not just from others, but from the very heart of God and the mission He's entrusted to us. When we become indifferent, we lose sight of the urgency and beauty of the Gospel. But the message of Christ is deeply relational. It's not about winning arguments—it's about welcoming people into God's family. To do that, we must see people as individuals, not as categories, issues, or labels.

It is love—not logic—that softens hearts and opens the door to truth. Evangelism begins by reengaging ourselves—emotionally, spiritually, and relationally—so we can connect with others in meaningful, Spirit-led ways.

Application

Ask God to give you a second touch—to see people the way He sees them. Start seeing names, not categories. Pray for specific individuals.

Break through apathy by intentionally connecting with others. Step out of your routine and into someone else's story. Relearn how to be present.

Reframe evangelism. It's not about duty—it's about invitation. It's not about pressure—it's about welcome. Ask the Lord to rekindle His heart in you. Reengage with the Gospel. Let it transform you again so you can carry it with compassion to others.

Reflection & Discussion Questions

1. In what ways has apathy crept into your spiritual life or witness?

2. How can you begin to reconnect with God's heart for people?

3. What are some relationships where God may be calling you to reengage?

4. How can you shift your mindset from evangelism as a duty to evangelism as invitation?

5. Who in your life needs to be seen, heard, and invited home?

———

The Messengers

God doesn't just send a message—He sends people. That means He sends *you*. This section is about understanding our identity as messengers of the Gospel. We're not just talking about trained speakers or missionaries—we're talking about everyday believers who reflect Jesus in the way they live, love, and listen.

These chapters will challenge you to move beyond hesitation and step fully into your role as His ambassador. You'll discover how to get equipped, confront your fears, and walk with integrity as someone sent by God. You don't need to be flawless. You just need to be faithful.

Section Three
Understanding People

Chapter 14
Understanding People

People judge by outward appearance, but the Lord looks at the heart. –
1 Samuel 16:7 (NLT)

*He comforts us in all our troubles so that we can comfort others. When
they are troubled, we will be able to give them the same comfort God has
given us. –* 2 Corinthians 1:4 (NLT)

"We are not here to win debates; we are here to win hearts."

———

You never know what God is doing in someone's heart. Don't give up.
Don't assume. Just listen, love, and share Jesus.

Why Understanding Matters

All the strategies, systems, and scripts in the world can't bring someone
to Christ. Only the Holy Spirit can draw a heart. That truth grounds
everything we do in evangelism. Our role is to love, listen, and speak
truth with compassion. His role is to open hearts.

People all over the world—rich and poor, educated and illiterate, in every
culture—have greeted our teams with warmth and sincerity. "Welcome.
We are so happy to have your outreach team at our church," they say.
"We've planned some service projects and sightseeing." But then often
comes the caution: "We don't want you to be disappointed. The people
here are just so hard."

We've heard that same message echoed in dozens of countries and
churches. These dear hosts meant well, and they were being honest. But

their words revealed something deeper: they had stopped expecting God to move. It affected their faith, their preparation, and their willingness to believe for breakthrough.

Yet again and again, we were surprised. In every imaginable circumstance, God had gone before us. Divine appointments unfolded, hearts opened, and lives were touched. Many of those who doubted later confessed, often with embarrassment, how little faith they had—and how amazed they were at what God had done. They had not because they asked not.

During my freshman year of college, I was one of those seemingly "hard" people. I was far from the Lord, wrestling with doubts and ready to walk away from the faith I had grown up with. My friend Ginny gently encouraged me to reconsider. She prayed for me, though I didn't know it at the time. One evening, we sat in her dorm room for hours while I voiced every question, doubt, and frustration I could muster.

Ginny listened patiently and tried to respond as best she could. Her roommate, who wasn't a believer, kept walking in and out of the room, overhearing our discussion. Later, I found out she told Ginny, "You are wasting your time with that girl. She's just trying to stump you. I'm not interested in becoming a Christian, but she's much worse than me."

On the surface, I may have looked prideful, cynical, and uninterested. But inside, I was searching for answers, longing for someone to show genuine care and patience.

A few months later, I had a powerful encounter with Jesus and surrendered my life to Him. I never looked back. Ginny's time and faithfulness were not wasted. That night taught me that you never really know what's going on beneath the surface.

Someone might say, "Don't bother—she'll never make it." But God sees what we cannot. I was that girl people thought was a waste of time. And yet, I encountered Jesus in an unexpected place—at the musical Hair. That's how far God will go to reach a searching heart.

Understanding people starts with seeing past the surface. Jesus modeled this. He related to people differently based on where they were—emotionally, spiritually, culturally. He spoke their language, met them on their turf, and always aimed at the heart. Sometimes pain came before sin, sometimes sin came before pain—but the answer was always the same: Jesus.

We must keep our focus on Jesus and avoid the smoke screens and distractions that try to sidetrack us. The goal isn't to win arguments. The goal is to win hearts, to comfort others with the comfort we've received, and to walk with people as they take steps toward Him.

Lessons Learned

Evangelism isn't about making judgments based on outward appearances—it's about trusting that God is always at work in the unseen places of the heart. It is the Holy Spirit who draws people to Himself; our role is simply to be faithful in showing up, speaking truth, and loving well.

Sometimes, what appears to be a hard heart is actually a hungry heart, covered by layers of hurt or disappointment. That's why we must never underestimate the quiet power of patience, prayer, and consistent presence. Jesus tailored His message to everyone He encountered, meeting them where they were—and we're called to do the same.

Application

Ask God to open your eyes to the hearts behind the faces. Refuse to write anyone off.

Lean into the Holy Spirit. Pray expectantly before every outreach. Ask God to lead you to those He has already been working on.

Take time to listen to people's stories. Engage with compassion, not conclusions.

Focus on Jesus. Avoid getting caught in distractions or debates. Speak truth in love and let God handle the outcome.

Reflection & Discussion Questions

1. Have you ever judged someone as uninterested, only to realize later they were searching?

2. Why do you think people often assume their community is "too hard" to reach?

3. How can you grow in sensitivity to the Holy Spirit when talking to others?

4. What can you do to better understand people's stories and needs?

5. Who in your life might need a second look—a second touch of understanding and love?

Chapter 15
Building Bridges

"You are the light of the world. A city on a hill cannot be hidden. Neither do people light a lamp and put it under a bowl. Instead, they put it on its stand, and it gives light to everyone in the house. In the same way, let your light shine before men, that they may see your good deeds and praise your Father in heaven." – Matthew 5:14–16 (NIV)

That you may prove yourselves to be blameless and innocent, children of God above reproach in the midst of a crooked and perverse generation, among whom you appear as lights in the world. – Philippians 2:15 (NASB)

For 'WHOEVER WILL CALL ON THE NAME OF THE LORD WILL BE SAVED.' How then will they call on Him in whom they have not believed? How will they believe in Him whom they have not heard? And how will they hear without a preacher? – Romans 10:13–14 (NASB)

"If we want to reach people no one else is reaching, we must go where no one else is going and love how no one else is loving."

———

You don't have to cross an ocean to build a bridge. Just cross the street—and let the light of Jesus shine.

Principles for Building Bridges

1. Know and Love the Lord

Your love for people flows from your love for God. When you know His heart, you care about what breaks it. The lost are not statistics—they are individuals whom God misses deeply.

2. Be Normal

Build genuine relationships with people—those who don't yet follow Jesus. Call them by name—Mary, John, Paul, Rebecca—not "the lost." If Jesus is central to your life, He'll come up naturally in conversations. Your life will speak volumes even before your words do.

3. Share Your Life and Open Your Mouth

Your lifestyle is a testimony, but you also need to speak up. Let people see your faith in action. Start conversations. Ask questions. Be real.

4. Go to Their World

Don't wait for people to come to your church or Bible study. Go to their turf. Build relationships where they are. Enter their world: their language, their culture, their concerns.

5. Start With Their Agenda

The things that made people lost have also made them ready. People are searching for meaning, healing, and hope. Listen to their felt needs: stress, loneliness, pain, fear, brokenness. If you meet them where they are, you can point them to the One who brings healing.

Sin (cause) = pain (result) = Jesus (cure)

Speak to the pain. Then point to the cure.

6. Focus on Jesus

Avoid distractions like denominational differences or political arguments. Stay focused on Jesus and His message. As Paul wrote in 1 Corinthians 2:2: "For I resolved to know nothing while I was with you except Jesus Christ and him crucified."

Let the Gospel remain simple, sincere, and Spirit-empowered.

How to Share Your Testimony

Listen carefully to people's stories. Ask thoughtful questions that invite conversation. Share your story authentically. Focus on how Jesus changed your life. Relate to their journey, not just their issues.

Lessons Learned

Evangelism is not about hitting numbers or fulfilling a quota—it's about building real relationships. People need to feel genuinely loved and valued before they will care about what you believe.

A consistent, Christ-centered life often speaks louder than words, becoming a steady witness to God's transforming power. When we're willing to meet people where they are—on their turf, in their context—we build trust and create space for authentic conversations. In the end, Jesus is both the message we carry and the bridge that connects hearts to the Father.

Application

Make a list of people you see regularly who don't know Jesus. Ask God to give you opportunities to build bridges. Be intentional in relationships. Don't retreat—engage.

Pray for God to open doors and give you the words to say. Be the light. Let your life shine in a way that makes others curious.

Reflection & Discussion Questions

1. Who are you intentionally building a bridge toward?

2. What's keeping you from stepping into someone else's world?

3. How can you listen more deeply to people's felt needs?

4. In what ways does your life reflect Jesus to your friends?

5. How can you share your story in a way that better connects?

Chapter 16
Seekers – Finding the Searching Heart

So that they should seek the Lord, in the hope that they might grope for Him and find Him, though He is not far from each one of us. – Acts 17:27 (NKJV)

"God is already working in the hearts of people—you just might be the answer to someone's prayer."

———

God is not far from anyone—and He often sends you to bridge the gap. Stay ready. Stay sensitive. The seekers are everywhere.

Laura and the Longing Heart

All around us, there are people seeking to know the Lord. The Holy Spirit has already been drawing them. Life's challenges, personal crises, and moments of curiosity often bring people to a place where they begin to ask deeper questions and search for truth.

Some start that search by dusting off an old Bible, typing a question into Google, or calling a friend they know is a believer. Across the world, millions are searching daily for answers about God, purpose, and peace. And we get the opportunity to walk with them on that journey of faith.

During a Joshua Generation training week in Concord, New Hampshire, we were preparing a team of teenagers to attend YWAM's Target World outreach at the 1996 Olympics in Atlanta. One afternoon, I dropped off a van load of teens at the public pool on Mountain Road.

When I walked through the gate, I noticed a group of our boys lined up against the wall. I approached a lifeguard nearby. "Hi, I'm the leader of this group. I see some of our teens are taking a break. Is everything okay?"

The lifeguard, a young woman named Laura, smiled. "Nothing major—they just needed to settle down. But you know," she added with a twinkle in her eye, "these kids are different. They're Christians, aren't they?"

I nodded, explaining they were preparing for an outreach. "They'll be doing street drama, dance, and sharing their testimonies."

She paused, then asked, "Can you come back at the end of my shift at 4:00 and talk to me about Jesus?"

When I returned, she was already waiting at a picnic table. On a prompting, I brought a brand-new Bible with me, still in its box.

"Deb," she said, "I've been longing to know the Lord. I even bought a small Bible at the grocery store, but the print is so tiny I can't read it. I just want to know what it says."

For the next hour, I shared my testimony, explained the Gospel, and answered her questions. When she prayed to receive Jesus, I gave her the new Bible. With tears streaming down her cheeks, she clutched it like a treasure.

She asked how she could grow in her faith and find a church. "I live in Goffstown," she said.

"I live in Goffstown too," I replied. "We have a weekly home meeting right in the center of town."

She looked stunned. "I live across the street from there. I can't believe this! I prayed that someone would come and tell me about God. And here you are. What are the odds?"

Lessons Learned

God is often working in people's hearts long before we ever arrive on the scene. While someone may seem indifferent or closed off on the outside, they could be quietly longing for hope on the inside.

When we listen to the Holy Spirit and remain sensitive to His leading, divine appointments unfold—often in the most unexpected ways. Simply being available and obedient can open the door to life-changing moments. The beauty of the Gospel is that it meets people right where they are—in the ordinary places of life, through everyday conversations, carried by those willing to be used.

Application

Be sensitive to the people around you. Ask God to make you aware of the seekers in your path. Pray for divine appointments—those moments when God connects you with someone already searching.

Be ready to share your testimony, answer questions, and offer help. Carry a Bible or a resource you can give away. Be prepared to walk with someone through their journey.

Keep your heart open—you may be the very person someone is praying for.

Reflection & Discussion Questions

1. Have you ever encountered someone who was already seeking God before you spoke with them?

2. What are some signs that someone might be spiritually open or searching?

3. How can you better prepare yourself for divine appointments?

4. Who in your life might be quietly searching for truth?

5. What's one way you can be more available and attentive to seekers this week?

Chapter 17
Open Hearts – Building Real Friendships

The Word became flesh and blood, and moved into the neighborhood. We saw the glory with our own eyes, the one-of-a-kind glory, like Father, like Son, generous inside and out, true from start to finish. – John 1:14 (The Message)

"They may not be ready to hear the Gospel, but they might be ready to hear your story."

———

People are longing to see that Jesus is real. Let them see Him in you—through friendship, authenticity, and love.

Sarah's Journey Toward Jesus

The non-Christian world needs to see a visible, authentic representation of what it truly means to follow Jesus. Sadly, many people's understanding of Christianity is shaped by media stereotypes, cultural distortions, or compromised examples. What they need most is to meet a Christian—up close—who is walking with Jesus in honesty, humility, and love.

One of the biggest challenges for believers is isolation. Within eighteen months of becoming a Christian, most people lose meaningful relationships with non-Christians. We often find ourselves saved, delivered, and then isolated.

But Jesus didn't isolate Himself. He came to reach lost people—and how did He do it? He moved into the neighborhood.

This was exactly the case with Sarah. One afternoon, she knocked on the door of our ministry home in Boston. "Hi, I'm Sarah. I walk past this house all the time. Is it a church?"

"Not exactly," I replied. "It's part of Youth With A Mission—we train missionaries and share the Gospel here in Boston and around the world. Come in!"

Sarah explained that she had been wondering about Christianity. She didn't know any Christians and had started reading the Bible and watching Christian TV shows. That simple visit turned into months of tea-time chats, questions, and growing friendship. She wasn't ready for a full Gospel presentation at first—but she was ready for relationship.

One day, I invited a few of our YWAM friends to join a visit with Sarah. We shared worship, testimonies, and fellowship. She was moved—deeply touched by the realness of it all. Eventually, she came to faith in Jesus, and her transformation began. She saw Christianity in action before she ever decided to follow Christ.

Lessons Learned

Many non-Christians are more open to building a relationship than engaging in a direct Gospel conversation. What people often need most is to see the Christian life lived out authentically and up close.

Jesus is best revealed not through pressure or performance, but through relationships built on love, transparency, and trust. Your life—your struggles, your victories, and your growth—can reflect Christ to someone who's quietly watching and wondering. Real friendship isn't about fixing people; it's about loving them the way Jesus does—faithfully, patiently, and without condition.

Application

Break out of the Christian bubble. Rebuild relationships with non-believers. Invite them into your life, your space, and your community.

Let your life be "show and tell"—where people can see what following Jesus really looks like.

Don't be afraid of your imperfections. God uses real people—not perfect ones—to display His grace. Ask God for opportunities to befriend someone who is curious but not yet convinced. Love them well.

Reflection & Discussion Questions

1. Are you currently building relationships with non-Christians? Why or why not?

2. What has kept you from letting others see your life up close?

3. How might you create space in your life for meaningful connection with seekers?

4. Why is relationship so powerful in communicating the Gospel?

5. Who in your life might be open to friendship—even if not yet open to faith?

Chapter 18
Looking for Truth – Conversations That Matter

And this continued for two years, so that all who dwelt in Asia heard the word of the Lord Jesus, both Jews and Greeks. – Acts 19:10 (NKJV)

For I am not ashamed of the gospel of Christ, for it is the power of God to salvation for everyone who believes, for the Jew first and also for the Greek. For in it the righteousness of God is revealed from faith to faith; as it is written, "The just shall live by faith." – Romans 1:16–17 (NKJV)

"Jesus is not just a good answer—He is the Truth people are searching for."

———

People are searching. You may be the one who helps them find the Truth they've been looking for.

Mary's Long Search for Answers

Jesus said He is the way, the truth, and the life. And truth seekers—those longing to understand the meaning of life—are all around us. They may not start with a desire for a Savior, but many are asking the right questions: Where did I come from? Why am I here? What happens when I die? Why is there so much pain and evil in the world?

That's how my friendship with Mary began. We had known each other in high school, but now we were both students on the same college campus. One day she approached me and said, "I heard you were a Christian. I have some questions."

Our conversation that evening went on for hours. Each question started with, "What does the Bible say about...?" After getting her answers, she abruptly said, "Okay, that's all for now," and left.

She wasn't necessarily looking for friendship—she was searching for truth. Several weeks later, she returned with more questions. I had answers to her earlier inquiries, and we continued.

This pattern repeated multiple times. One day, she came to me and said, "Do you have some time to talk? Thank you for all these moments of sharing. My questions went on and on, I know. You helped me understand the Gospel and gave me a foundation for trusting Jesus. I am here tonight to pray with you to give my life to Jesus."

That moment was fifty years ago—and Mary is still walking with the Lord today. Her life was completely transformed. She found the truth, and the truth set her free. The Gospel really is the power of God for salvation.

Lessons Learned

Those who are truly seeking truth often begin with deep, difficult questions that don't always have easy answers. That's why it's so important to give people space to ask, to process, and to reflect without pressure or judgment.

The Bible offers clear, life-giving answers to the biggest questions people wrestle with, but our role isn't to have all the answers—it's to walk alongside others as they discover them. We may not know everything, but we can help others find the truth that changes lives. And that truth is not just found in our opinions or experiences—it's found in the Gospel itself.

Application

Pay attention to the questions people ask—they often reveal a deeper spiritual search.

Commit to being a learner yourself. Grow in your understanding of Scripture and be prepared to engage thoughtfully.

Point people to Jesus and the Word of God—not just your experiences.

Introduce others to trusted resources and teachers who can help them explore apologetics and biblical truth. Give people time. Don't rush the process. Count it a joy to walk with someone as they seek the truth.

Reflection & Discussion Questions

1. What big life questions have you heard from others recently?

2. How do you typically respond when someone brings up a difficult question about faith?

3. What resources have helped you better understand your faith and explain it to others?

4. Why is it important to let people count the cost of following Jesus?

5. Who in your life may be searching for truth right now?

Chapter 19
Unaware – Introducing Jesus to the Unknowing

Then Paul stood in the midst of the Areopagus and said, 'Men of Athens, I perceive that in all things you are very religious; for as I was passing through and considering the objects of your worship, I even found an altar with this inscription: TO THE UNKNOWN GOD. Therefore, the One whom you worship without knowing, Him I proclaim to you: God, who made the world and everything in it, since He is Lord of heaven and earth, does not dwell in temples made with hands. Nor is He worshiped with men's hands, as though He needed anything, since He gives to all life, breath, and all things. And He has made from one blood every nation of men to dwell on all the face of the earth, and has determined their preappointed times and the boundaries of their dwellings, so that they should seek the Lord, in the hope that they might grope for Him and find Him, though He is not far from each one of us; for in Him we live and move and have our being, as also some of your own poets have said, "For we are also His offspring. – Acts 17:22–28 (NKJV)

"People don't know what they don't know—until someone lives it in front of them."

———

Many people don't know what they're missing until they see Jesus in someone else. Be that someone.

A Grocery Line Encounter

In today's post-Christian Western culture, many people have never read the Bible or heard the message of Jesus. A generation ago, basic biblical literacy was assumed. Now, people often grow up without ever attending church, praying before meals, or understanding what sin and salvation mean.

Instead of responding to guilt over sin, many are navigating pain caused by the consequences of decisions made apart from God's truth. When there's a spiritual vacuum, people redefine truth based on what feels right. When pain hits, they don't know where to turn for healing.

This is why it's important to meet people at their point of need, not just their point of failure.

While raising four teenagers, I found myself at the grocery store nearly every day. I often prayed for opportunities to connect with the cashiers. Diane was one of them. Even when her line was the longest, I always waited for her. She recognized me.

"You and your husband are in here all the time. Kids, right?" she said with a grin.

One day, Diane's usual smile was gone. Her eyes were red. I gently asked, "Are you okay?"

"No, my mother is dying."

I reached out and said, "Mine too. I visited her this week. I'm so sorry."

She invited me to return during her break. We sat down, and I shared how Jesus was my comfort. Diane said she had never gone to church, never owned a Bible. Her openness in pain allowed me to introduce her to the Lord.

Our friendship grew from that moment. I continued choosing her line, and she knew I cared.

On another outreach, we sang "Father Abraham" with a group of children. When we asked if they knew who Abraham was, one child guessed, "A president of the United States?"

That response revealed the depth of biblical disconnection. In a culture that no longer knows the stories of Scripture, we must patiently live them out and build relationships where our faith can be seen and shared.

Lessons Learned

Many people today have never truly encountered who Jesus is or what the Bible actually teaches. In a world filled with noise and confusion, pain often becomes the doorway that truth alone cannot unlock. That's why the Gospel must not only be preached—it must be lived.

Though biblical literacy may be low, spiritual hunger remains, quietly present beneath the surface. In these moments, it's often our presence, our love, and our willingness to listen that begin to open hearts to the Good News. People need to see the Gospel embodied before they're ready to embrace it.

Application

Ask God to make you aware of those around you who don't yet know Jesus. Look for moments of pain or need where God can shine through your compassion.

Be patient. Understand that people unfamiliar with Scripture may take longer to grasp spiritual truths.

Focus less on correcting and more on connecting. Let people see Jesus through your actions before they understand Him through your words.

Keep showing up. In the grocery line, in the classroom, in your neighborhood—be a consistent presence that reflects Christ.

Reflection & Discussion Questions

1. Who in your daily life might be unaware of who Jesus truly is?

2. How can you reflect God's love in ways that open hearts?

3. What assumptions about people's spiritual background might you need to let go of?

4. How do you patiently walk with someone who doesn't yet know the Bible?

5. What are simple ways you can live the Gospel in front of others?

Chapter 20
Hostile – Reaching the Hurt and Resistant

Do not be overcome by evil but overcome evil with good. – Romans 12:21 (NIV)

"Love disarms what logic cannot."

―――――

Love doesn't argue. It listens, it learns, and it leads the way. Let love speak first.

A Flight with Godfred

I made my way through the 747 plane and found my seat in the middle section. The gentleman seated next to me greeted me with a nod. The nine-hour flight to Poland would go faster with some friendly conversation, I thought. We introduced ourselves.

"Nice to meet you, Godfred. Are you traveling to Warsaw to visit or do business?"

"I am a professor from Austria and have been lecturing in the United States for the past few weeks. I will be heading home after a week in Poland."

"What is your field of expertise?"

"Brain chemistry."

This wasn't a topic I was familiar with, so I followed up with, "Is there a main point to your lectures?"

He seemed eager to share. "All of life is about brain chemistry. If you have good chemistry, you have a good life. If you don't, you won't."

I nodded, not that I agreed, but that I understood his point.

"What brings you to Poland?" he inquired.

"I am with a group on a mission trip. We will be teaching young leaders and sharing the Gospel."

I thought this was an open door for conversation for the rest of the flight. I was wrong.

"Oh, you are a Christian. Please, let's agree to not talk about religion on this flight. I really do not care for that kind of conversation."

That was blunt. Our friendly exchange now had a chilly atmosphere. I was silently praying and listening for the Holy Spirit's nudging.

"Will you see your family soon?" I asked.

He was comfortable with a conversation about family and proceeded to tell me about his wife and children. I responded the same, except I shared with him about meeting our son after fourteen years of separation and the amazing way we were able to find each other.

"One day we didn't know each other, and the next we were sitting and sharing our lives with each other."

"Well, that is an amazing story. It was a miracle how that happened," he said.

"Yes. I have had some miracles happen in my life. When I was a sophomore in college, I was not a religious person, but I made a decision to trust Jesus with my life."

He seemed interested now, and the hostility that I felt before had diminished.

"My life drastically changed," I continued. "Before that, I was confused and struggling with depression. After that, I had hope and a changed heart. Everything about my life changed."

"That's a miracle!" he replied again.

"About your earlier comment about brain chemistry, I think my brain chemistry was the same, but my heart changed, and that changed my life," I said.

That comment seemed to close the door again. He picked up a book and started reading. Then to my surprise, he said, "I have had some unexplainable miracles in my life too."

For the next hour, he shared experiences with me where he was aware that something supernatural had happened, how his life was spared, or how he had some opportunity that changed his life. I eventually was able to share the Gospel with him clearly, and he understood. When our plane landed, we were still engaged in conversation, and he thanked me for the things we spoke about.

"God must have a purpose for your life. You can see that He even sent me here to sit next to you."

He gave me a nod. It was the first step toward opening his heart to Jesus.

Lessons Learned

What appears as hostility on the surface is often a cover for deep hurt or past disappointment. When someone resists the Gospel, it doesn't always mean rejection—it might mean they've been wounded before. In those moments, love, patience, and the sharing of our personal stories can do more than arguments ever will.

Listening builds trust, disarms defensiveness, and shows genuine care. It's okay if the message takes time to reach the heart—evangelism is often a journey, not a single moment. A gentle, Spirit-led approach can open doors that forceful debate never could, allowing the love of Christ to break through.

Application

Pray for the Holy Spirit's guidance when speaking to someone who seems hostile.

Look for common ground—shared experiences, struggles, or values. Be patient. Don't press the issue, but gently plant seeds of truth and love. Let your own transformation speak for itself. Testimonies often reach where arguments cannot.

Remember: It's not your job to win an argument. It's your job to love well.

Reflection & Discussion Questions

1. Have you ever felt shut down in a spiritual conversation? How did you respond?

2. What do you think causes some people to become hostile toward Christianity?

3. How can you reflect love in the face of resistance?

4. What role does your story play in helping others open up?

5. Who in your life may be closed off, but still watching how you live?

_____

Understanding People

If we want to reach people, we must really see them. This section is an invitation to slow down and ask deeper questions—not just about methods, but about hearts. Jesus was a master at this. He knew what was hiding behind people's words, behind their anger, pain, and silence. These chapters will help you look past appearances and listen with spiritual ears. You'll learn to recognize the questions people aren't asking out loud, and how to speak the Gospel in a way that meets them where they are. Evangelism starts with compassion—and that's something we can all grow in.

Section Four
Our Message

Chapter 21
The Benefits of Salvation

This is good and pleasing in the sight of God our Savior, who wants everyone to be saved and to come to the knowledge of the truth. – 1 Timothy 2:3–4

"The Gospel doesn't just save us from something; it saves us for something."

———

When I first encountered the Gospel, I thought salvation meant only going to heaven after I died. But as I began to grow in my relationship with Jesus, I realized I had received far more than a future destination—I had been given a new identity, a new purpose, and new power for life.

One day while reading the Scriptures, I saw how many benefits mine were already: peace, joy, purpose, and the presence of the Holy Spirit. I wasn't just rescued from darkness—I was invited into God's family. I had passed from death to life, and now I had a reason to live.

That realization changed everything. Evangelism was no longer a duty. It became an invitation to share the incredible gift I had received.

Lessons Learned

Salvation is more than forgiveness. It is the full work of God to restore us from the inside out. Here are just some of the spiritual benefits:

Romans 1:16 – The Gospel is the power of God for salvation

2 Corinthians 5:17 – We are made new; old things pass away

2 Corinthians 3:15–18 – The veil is lifted; we are transformed

John 1:12 – We become children of God

John 5:24 – We pass from death to life

Ephesians 1:13–14 – We are sealed with the Holy Spirit and receive His power

Romans 8:15–17 – We are heirs of God and joint heirs with Christ

2 Peter 1:4 – We take on the divine nature

Psalm 119:11 – We can treasure *God's Word* to avoid sin

Romans 8:28 – All things work together for good

John 10:27–30 – We know His voice, and He gives us eternal life

Philippians 4:19 – He supplies our needs and calls us to a great purpose

2 Corinthians 5:17–20 – We are given the ministry of reconciliation and made His ambassadors

Application

Take time to reflect on your personal journey. The more we understand what we've received in Christ, the more grateful—and bold—we become in sharing it.

Your testimony is not only what God saved you from, but also what He brought you into. Peace. Identity. Purpose. Power. That's worth telling the world about.

Reflection & Discussion Questions

1. Which of the benefits of salvation listed above is most meaningful to you right now, and why?

2. How has your understanding of salvation changed over time?

3. How would you explain the "power of the Gospel" to someone new in faith?

4. In what ways do you see your identity as a child of God affecting your daily life?

5. Who in your life needs to hear about the benefits of salvation? What's one step you can take to share with them?

Chapter 22
Prayer and Evangelism

Then he said to his disciples, "The harvest is plentiful but the workers are few. Ask the Lord of the harvest, therefore, to send out workers into his harvest field." – Matthew 9:37–38 (NIV)

I urge, then, first of all, that petitions, prayers, intercession and thanksgiving be made for all people. – 1 Timothy 2:1 (NIV)

Moreover, as for me, far be it from me that I should sin against the Lord by ceasing to pray for you. And I will instruct you in the good and right way. – 1 Samuel 12:23 (ESV)

———

Let us begin with prayer—and watch what God will do.

We Begin With Prayer

Evangelism begins with prayer. Before we ever share the Gospel, before we speak a word, we go to the Lord. In Matthew 9:37–38, Jesus revealed the great need—many souls are ready to hear, but few are willing to go. His instruction was simple: PRAY. Ask the Lord to send laborers. Prayer is not optional; it is essential.

Prayer is the invisible power behind every visible movement of God. Paul echoed this urgency in 1 Timothy 2:1, urging us to pray for everyone, and in doing so, partner with God's will and mercy.

Faith vs. Fatalism

We must reject fatalism—the passive mindset that "whatever will be, will be." Scripture reveals a different truth: prayer changes things.

- Moses' intercession moved God to spare Israel (Exodus 32:9–14).
- Amos' prayers caused God to relent from sending disaster (Amos 7:1–6).
- Elijah prayed for fire and it came (1 Kings 18:36–38).
- Joshua prayed and the sun stood still (Joshua 10:12–13).

The earnest prayer of a righteous person has great power and produces wonderful results. – James 5:16 (NLT)

If two of you on earth agree about anything they ask for, it will be done for them by my Father in heaven. – Matthew 18:19 (NIV)

The Power and Purpose of Prayer in Evangelism

Prayer opens doors—both spiritual and practical. Before we speak to people about God, we must speak to God about people. We ask for open hearts, divine appointments, sensitivity to the Holy Spirit, and boldness to share.

- Prayer aligns us with God's heart.
- Prayer removes spiritual blindness (2 Corinthians 4:4).
- Prayer prepares us to walk in compassion and authority.
- Prayer leads us to specific people, places, and words.

"In prayer you align yourself to the purpose and power of God, and He is able to do things through you that would otherwise not happen." – Pastor Jack Hayford

Our Calling to Intercede

Every believer is called to pray for others.

Intercession: Standing in the gap for the lost, pleading for their salvation.

Supplication: Asking God to work in specific lives and situations.

Thanksgiving: Acknowledging God's mercy and faithfulness.

We must see intercession as love in action. It is not just prayer; it is spiritual warfare. We become partners with the Holy Spirit in rescuing people from darkness.

"All Christians have the ministry of reconciliation and the word of reconciliation."

Practical Prayer Guidelines

- **Begin with Praise** – Start by thanking God and recognizing who He is.
- **Invite the Holy Spirit** – Ask for guidance, boldness, and clarity.
- **Resist the Enemy** – Stand against fear, lies, and distractions.
- **Pray for Specific People** – Name your neighbors, coworkers, and friends who need Jesus.
- **Ask for Divine Appointments** – Pray to be in the right place at the right time.
- **Pray for Laborers** – Ask God to raise up others to share the Gospel.
- **Pray for Open Doors** – Trust God to make a way, even in the hardest hearts.

Lessons Learned

Prayer is not an optional add-on to evangelism—it's the foundation. Before a word is spoken or a conversation is had, prayer prepares the way. The results belong to God—the harvest is His responsibility—but prayer is ours. It aligns our hearts with His, softens the soil of those we'll encounter, and prepares us to speak with grace and boldness.

Prayer shapes both the messenger and the hearer, reminding us that we are not powerless in this mission. We have direct access to the Lord of the harvest, and through prayer, we join Him in the work He is already doing.

Application

Living a Life of Evangelistic Prayer

Start a prayer journal focused on unsaved friends and family. Set aside weekly times to intercede for your city, neighborhood, and nation. Join others in prayer for outreach efforts locally and globally.

Ask God daily for divine appointments. Pray before every conversation you hope will lead to a Gospel opportunity.

Reflection & Discussion Questions

1. Who are the three people in your life you are praying for to come to Jesus?

2. How have you seen prayer change a situation or open a door?

3. What keeps you from praying more consistently for the lost?

4. What practical steps can you take this week to make evangelistic prayer a priority?

Chapter 23
The Gospel Message – What Really Happens When People Receive Jesus

Yet to all who did receive him, to those who believed in his name, he gave the right to become children of God. – John 1:12 (NIV)

Everyone who calls on the name of the Lord will be saved. – Romans 10:13 (NIV)

———

God has given you the message of reconciliation. Will you speak it with courage and love?

The Heart of the Gospel

What really happens when someone receives Jesus? Beyond the prayer, beyond the moment—it's a supernatural transformation. The Gospel is more than a message; it is the power of God to bring salvation, restoration, and growth. The Holy Spirit initiates a divine exchange: sin for righteousness, separation for relationship, brokenness for healing.

Although every person's journey to Christ is unique, certain truths remain consistent. We are created for a relationship with God. Sin separates us from Him. There are consequences for that separation. But God, in His mercy, made a way—Jesus. Through His life, death, and resurrection, He provided the only path back to God. When we respond to this provision, we are restored and begin a journey of growth.

The Gospel Message

1. Relationship

We were created for relationship with God. He designed us to walk with Him, know Him, and be loved by Him. This relationship is our ultimate purpose.

"In the beginning God created..." – Genesis 1:1

"You have made us for Yourself, O Lord, and our hearts are restless until they rest in You." – Augustine

2. Separation

But sin entered the world. We chose independence, and with that came separation. Sin is not just doing wrong—it's the decision to live life without God.

"Your iniquities have separated you from your God..." – Isaiah 59:2

3. Consequences

The consequence of sin is death—spiritual death, separation from the life we were meant to live.

"For the wages of sin is death..." – Romans 6:23

"All have sinned and fall short of the glory of God." – Romans 3:23

4. Provision

Jesus is God's answer to our separation. He lived a perfect life, died in our place, and rose again to restore us.

"Christ died for sins once for all, the righteous for the unrighteous, to bring you to God." – 1 Peter 3:18

5. Response

We must respond by receiving Jesus—by faith, not by works. This is a decision of the heart, a surrender of control, a turning from sin.

"To all who received Him... He gave the right to become children of God." – John 1:12

"If you confess with your mouth, 'Jesus is Lord,' and believe in your heart... you will be saved." – Romans 10:9

6. Restoration and Growth and Discipleship

When we receive Jesus, we are not just saved—we are restored. And the journey continues as we grow in Him. This new life is marked by transformation, discipleship, and purpose.

"If anyone is in Christ, the new creation has come..." – 2 Corinthians 5:17

"He who began a good work in you will carry it on to completion..." – Philippians 1:6

The Wordless Book: A Simple Gospel Tool

This timeless tool has been used for generations to communicate the Gospel clearly and effectively, especially with children and visual learners. Each color represents a key element of the Gospel message:

- **Gold** – Heaven and God's Love

Gold represents the beauty and perfection of heaven—God's home. Revelation 21:21 describes heaven's streets as made of pure gold. Heaven is where God dwells, and His desire is for us to live with Him there. It is a place with no sorrow, pain, or death (Revelation 21:4). Jesus came that we might have abundant life—not just in eternity, but here and now (John 10:10).

Ask: "Would you like to go to heaven one day?"

- **Dark** – Sin and Separation

This color symbolizes the darkness of sin. Sin is anything we do that separates us from God. Romans 3:23 says that all have sinned and fall short of God's glory. Romans 6:23 reminds us that the wages of sin is death—spiritual separation from God. Without Jesus, we are spiritually lost, and no good work can make up for our sin.

Ask: "Have you ever done something you know was wrong?"

85

- **Red** – Jesus' Sacrifice

Red represents the blood of Jesus, shed for the forgiveness of our sins. While we were still sinners, Christ died for us (Romans 5:8). Jesus took our place, dying the death that we deserved, and offering us life in return. 1 Peter 3:18 says He died for the unrighteous to bring us to God. Through His death and resurrection, the way back to God is open.

Ask: "Do you know why Jesus died on the cross?"

- **White** – Cleansing and New Life

White signifies purity and forgiveness. When we receive Jesus, He washes us clean. Psalm 51:7 says, "Wash me and I will be whiter than snow." Our sins are forgiven, and we are made new (2 Corinthians 5:17). We can now walk in freedom and righteousness—not because of our efforts, but because of His grace.

Ask: "Would you like to be forgiven and made clean before God?"

- **Green** – Growth and Discipleship

Green represents growth. Just like grass and trees grow, we are meant to grow in our relationship with God. After salvation, we learn to pray, read the Bible, join a community of believers, and tell others about Jesus. Spiritual growth is a lifelong journey.

Ask: "Would you like to learn how to grow in your faith?"

This simple tool reminds us that the Gospel is not just a message to share—but a life to live.

Guiding Others to Christ: Key Question

"Has there ever been a time in your life when you personally asked Jesus to be your Savior and Lord?"

Lessons Learned

The Gospel was never meant to be merely informational—it's deeply relational. While we may present the truth with our words, it is the Holy Spirit who opens hearts and draws people to Christ. As we share, we must remember that people will respond in different ways, but the core message of hope and redemption never changes.

To faithfully present the Gospel, we must first understand its basic truths—who Jesus is, what He has done, and how people can respond. The Gospel is both simple and profound. It can be understood by a child, yet powerful enough to transform even the hardest heart. The Gospel is not just a message—it is the very power of God to change lives.

When we are grounded in this truth, we become powerful tools in His hands. And ultimately, it's not the perfection of our delivery that makes the difference, but the love, clarity, and Spirit-led compassion with which we share. Love makes the Gospel come alive.

Application

Walking Someone Through Salvation

- Listen well. Let them speak about their story, doubts, and questions.
- Share clearly. Use Scripture. Use the Wordless Book. Use your story.
- Invite sincerely. Ask, "Would you like to receive Jesus today?"
- Pray simply. Guide them through a heartfelt, honest prayer of salvation.
- Celebrate. Affirm their decision and remind them of God's promises.
- Encourage growth. Give them a Bible, connect them to a local church, and help them begin walking with Jesus daily.

Reflection & Discussion Questions

1. How would you explain the Gospel to someone in one minute?

2. What fears or hesitations do you have when sharing the message?

3. Have you ever used the Wordless Book? Would you be willing to try it?

4. Who in your life needs to hear this message soon?

5. What is one step you can take to grow in sharing the Gospel?

Chapter 24
Giving an Invitation

Now then, we are ambassadors for Christ, as though God were pleading through us: we implore you on Christ's behalf, be reconciled to God. – 2 Corinthians 5:20 (NKJV)

For with the heart one believes unto righteousness, and with the mouth confession is made unto salvation. – Romans 10:10 (NKJV)

"The Gospel is only good news if it gets there in time." – Carl F.H. Henry

"God is always at work, but He waits for us to extend the invitation."

"In a few minutes, I'm going to ask you to respond." – Billy Graham

———

Who might be waiting for you to ask, "Would you like to receive Jesus today?"

The Power of Invitation

The Gospel demands a response. When we share the Good News of Jesus, we must also lovingly and boldly invite people to respond to Him. We are not just proclaiming information—we are offering the opportunity for transformation. The invitation is not our own, but God's. As His ambassadors, we are pleading with people on Christ's behalf: "Be reconciled to God."

When we invite people to follow Jesus, we give them a moment in time to say yes to eternity. We join with the Holy Spirit, who has already been drawing their hearts. Sometimes, all it takes is a clear invitation for someone to step into new life.

Biblical Examples of Invitation

- **Peter at Pentecost** – After preaching the Gospel, Peter called the crowd to "Repent and be baptized..." (Acts 2:38). That day, 3,000 people responded.
- **Jesus' Own Words** – "Come to Me, all you who labor and are heavy laden, and I will give you rest" (Matthew 11:28).
- **Old Testament Calls** – "Choose this day whom you will serve" (Joshua 24:15); "Who is on the Lord's side?" (Exodus 32:26).
- **Paul's Plea** – "We implore you on Christ's behalf: Be reconciled to God" (2 Corinthians 5:20).

Real-Life Stories of Invitation

Mary at the Nursing Home

During an outreach to a nursing home, our team shared the Gospel using the Wordless Book. We told the residents that we would give them an opportunity to pray with us at the end. Mary, a 99-year-old woman, was fully alert and deeply engaged. When I asked if she wanted to trust Jesus as her Lord and Savior, her face lit up with joy.

"Of course," she said, tears in her eyes. "I've been waiting all my life for someone to come and tell me how to become a Christian. This is the best day of my life!"

She had waited a lifetime for an invitation.

Krakow, Poland

A large crowd gathered in the Main Square to watch our Gospel drama. As I shared the message, I prepared them throughout by saying, "In a few minutes, I'm going to invite you to respond to what you've seen."

I explained how the character in the drama represented all of us—drawn into sin and brokenness, yet pursued by Jesus who offers forgiveness and restoration. When the invitation was given, many raised their hands and were led in a prayer of salvation.

Our team followed up with personal conversations, and people were connected with local churches. The key was simple: give people a clear moment to say yes to Jesus.

Lessons from Dr. Ralph Bell

At a Billy Graham Evangelism training, Dr. Ralph Bell emphasized the importance of preparing people to respond. He highlighted how Billy Graham would repeatedly say, "In a few minutes, I'm going to ask you to make a decision to follow Jesus."

This approach helped listeners understand that a response was coming and that the Gospel required something of them. It created space for the Holy Spirit to work and gave clarity to the moment of decision. This training shifted how I shared Christ—and how I invited others to Him.

Lessons Learned

Sometimes, what people need most is simply to be asked.

An open, heartfelt invitation can be the turning point in someone's spiritual journey. But how we extend that invitation matters—it should be made with clarity, compassion, and a sense of urgency rooted in love.

The Holy Spirit often moves powerfully when we create space for people to respond. We can't assume they automatically know they need to act on what they've just heard. That's why it's important to be clear, intentional, and even repetitive. A well-timed invitation, given more than once, can break through hesitation and open the door to life-changing decisions.

Application

How to Give an Invitation

- **Prepare the listener** – Mention early on that you will be giving them a chance to respond.
- **Be clear** – Share the Gospel simply and understandably.

- **Be bold** – Ask directly: "Would you like to receive Jesus as your Lord and Savior?"
- **Be patient** – If they're not ready, affirm their interest and stay connected.
- **Be prayerful** – Trust the Holy Spirit to do what only He can do.
- **Be available** – Follow up. Help them take the next steps in their new faith.

Reflection & Discussion Questions

1. Have you ever clearly invited someone to follow Jesus? What happened?

2. What stops you from offering an invitation?

3. How can you prepare someone for a response in future conversations?

4. Who in your life might be waiting for an invitation today?

5. What's one way you could improve how you give an invitation?

Chapter 25
Tell Your Story

In the future, when your children ask their fathers, "What is the meaning of these stones?" you are to tell them, "Israel crossed the Jordan on dry ground." – Joshua 4:21 (NIV)

We proclaim to you the one who existed from the beginning, whom we have heard and seen. We saw him with our own eyes and touched him with our own hands. He is the Word of life. – 1 John 1:1 (NLT)

"Come and listen, all you who fear God, and I will tell you what he did for me." – Psalm 66:16 (NLT)

They triumphed over him by the blood of the Lamb and by the word of their testimony; they did not love their lives so much as to shrink from death. – Revelation 12:11 (NIV)

"A man with an argument is always at the mercy of a man with an experience."

"Your testimony is the Gospel written in your life."

"Jesus changed me—and He can change you, too."

"Your story matters. Someone is waiting to hear it."

———

God gave you a story—now go and tell it. Testimonies are our love letters to the world, declaring the goodness of God.

Tell the story only you can tell—and let it lead others to the Savior who changed your life.

The Power of a Testimony

Sharing Our Stones of Remembrance

In Joshua 4, we encounter a powerful moment in Israel's journey where God commands His people to set up two monuments of stone. These stones were not just markers of time, but symbols of God's faithfulness and power.

As the Israelites crossed the Jordan River on dry ground, God instructed Joshua to gather twelve stones from the riverbed—one for each tribe—to build a monument at Gilgal. These stones would serve as a reminder of the miraculous way in which God led His people into the promised land.

Joshua told the Israelites, "In the future, when your children ask their fathers, 'What is the meaning of these stones?' you are to tell them, 'Israel crossed the Jordan on dry ground'" (Joshua 4:21-22). These stones were meant to be a witness to future generations, a teaching tool to show how God had worked in the past, so they could trust Him in the present and future. Just as the Israelites used the stones to remember God's power and provision, we, too, are called to share our personal stories and testimonies of God's faithfulness with those around us.

Our testimonies act as stones of remembrance—moments in our lives where we have seen God's hand move in powerful ways. These stories remind us of God's presence and power, and when we share them, they not only strengthen our own faith but also serve as a beacon to others. Just as the Israelites would rely on their stones in times of trial or doubt, our testimonies can inspire those who are facing their own "giants" or moments of need.

In the same way that Joshua's monument was a physical marker, our personal testimonies are spiritual markers. When we share them, we not only witness to the faithfulness of God in our own lives but also inspire others to trust in God's provision and strength. Whether in moments of triumph or trial, these stories stand as powerful reminders that God is always with us, working for our good.

This chapter will explore the importance of sharing our testimonies and how they can serve as powerful tools for building faith, fostering hope, and encouraging others to trust in God. Just as the Israelites carried those stones with them into the promised land, we carry our stories to testify of God's greatness and love, ensuring that the next generation hears of His mighty works.

Proclaiming the One Who Changed Us

Your testimony is a living witness. It proclaims the transforming power of Jesus Christ through your life. People can argue theology, but they cannot argue with your story. It is one of the most powerful ways you can share the Gospel—by telling how Jesus made you new.

John, one of Jesus' closest followers, wrote, "We proclaim to you the one we have seen and heard." That's what a testimony is—proclaiming the One who changed us.

Why Your Testimony Matters

2 Corinthians 1:3–4 reminds us that the comfort we receive from God is meant to be shared. Your story is a bridge—connecting your personal encounter with Jesus to the person in front of you who may be longing for hope. God doesn't waste any part of our story. The pain, the joy, the journey—it all points to Him.

When you share what Jesus has done in your life, it opens the door for others to see what He might do in theirs.

The Three Phases of a Testimony

- **Before Christ** – Who were you before Jesus? What were your struggles, fears, or beliefs?
- **Encounter with Christ** – How did you come to know Him? What led to your decision?
- **Life After Christ** – What has changed? How is your life different today?

Keep it simple, sincere, and focused on the transformation. People relate to real life.

How to Share Your Testimony Effectively

- **Listen First** – Ask questions and listen for ways your story might connect to theirs.
- **Be Authentic** – Don't exaggerate or make it sound perfect. Be real.
- **Use Everyday Language** – Avoid Christian phrases or religious jargon.
- **Keep it Short** – A 3- to 5-minute version of your testimony is a great starting point.
- **Point to Jesus** – It's not about how bad you were, but how good He is.
- **Practice** – Write it out. Share it with friends. Be ready when the opportunity comes.

Your Testimony as Evidence

Today's culture often values personal experience as truth. Your testimony is a powerful witness that Jesus is real and active. While our stories can deeply connect with others, we always point people to the greater truth of God's Word.

When sharing:

To the religious: emphasize grace and relationship, not performance (Galatians 2:15–16).

To the broken: highlight freedom and healing through Christ (Matthew 11:28-30)

Real-Life Examples

The Power of a Changed Life

"One thing I know: that though I was blind, now I see." – John 9:25 (NKJV)

"I was one way, and now I am completely different. And the thing that happened in between was Him." – Mary Magdalene (The Chosen)

Donna, a college classmate, experienced radical transformation after accepting Jesus. Her friends were stunned. They asked her, "What happened to you?" She didn't have a deep theological answer. She just smiled and said, "I finally know I'm loved, and I know who I belong to." Her life spoke louder than any sermon.

Lessons Learned

Your testimony is more than just your story—it's a bridge between someone else's need and God's grace. While God works uniquely in every life, all testimonies ultimately point to the same Savior.

A real, honest, and relatable story can soften hearts and open doors to the Gospel in ways that arguments or theology alone cannot. You don't need to have all the answers or present a perfectly polished message. Just share what Jesus has done for you. That authentic witness, empowered by the Holy Spirit, carries the power to bring hope and transformation to someone who's searching.

Application

- Write your testimony down – Take time to reflect on your story and write it out using the three-part format (Before, Encounter, After). This will help you share it clearly and confidently.
- Practice telling it – Share it with a trusted friend or family member and ask for feedback.
- Pray for opportunities – Ask God to open doors for you to share your story and to prepare hearts to receive it.
- Adapt your story for different audiences – Keep a short (2–3 minute) version for casual conversations and a longer one for deeper talks.
- Point people to Jesus, not yourself – Your story is about what He has done.

Your testimony is not about how bad you were, but how good Jesus is.

Reflection & Discussion Questions

1. Have you ever shared your testimony with someone who wasn't a believer? What was the result?

2. Which parts of your story might connect with the people in your life?

3. What keeps you from sharing your story more often?

4. Who needs to hear what God has done for you?

5. How has your story grown or changed as your walk with Jesus has deepened?

Chapter 26
I Once Was Lost But Now I Am Found

The Power of a Tract: From Cal U to Nepal

Main Point: Every small act of sharing the Gospel, no matter how simple, can transform lives and bring lasting change.

Doug and I were caught off guard when we received a late-night call from Gary, someone we didn't immediately remember. But as he shared his story, it all came flooding back. Gary had been part of our early ministry at Cal U in Pennsylvania, where both Doug and I gave our lives to Jesus during the Jesus Movement of the 70s.

Back then, we sold hoagies on campus, slipping Gospel tracts into the wrapping, eager to share Jesus in any way we could. One day, Gary bought a sub, read the tract, and gave his life to Christ. He joined our fellowship, went on our first missions trip to Brazil, and has been a missionary and pastor for the last 38 years, continuing to share the Gospel with others.

Years later, I learned of Nick's mother in Nepal, who came to faith through reading a tract. Despite severe persecution, she boldly shared her faith, leading hundreds to Christ and starting two churches. Doug, Nick, and his mother continue to visit their Nepali friends, seeing hearts opened to the Gospel.

This reminded me of the power of simple acts of faith—whether it's a tract, a word of encouragement, or a conversation. These small seeds can make a lasting impact, transform lives and spread God's love. It truly matters how we share the Gospel, no matter how small the gesture may seem.

Scripture:

One who is faithful in a very little is also faithful in much. – Luke 16:10a (ESV)

A Daughter's Longing and the Father Who Never Left

Main Point: God is the Father we all long for, offering healing and restoration even in our deepest pain.

It was a cold January night in New York, with the wind biting through layers of clothing as we walked through the streets, offering warmth and food to the homeless. Our team from the church distributed blankets, hot drinks, and sandwiches, bringing hope to those finding shelter in doorways and makeshift homes.

As I turned a corner, I saw a young woman nestled between two store entryways, trying to make a home in the freezing cold. We offered her blankets and warm drinks, along with the message of God's love. She smiled but declined our offer to hear more about Jesus.

Before leaving, I asked, "Is there anything we can pray for you about?" There was a long pause before she looked me in the eyes and said, "Yes. Would you pray that I can find my father? I never knew him, he left my mother before I was born." The sadness in her voice was palpable, and I felt her deep longing for something more than just a change in circumstances.

As I closed my eyes to pray, I felt the still, small voice of God speaking to my heart: "I am the Father she longs for and needs." I shared these words with her, telling her that although her earthly father had abandoned her, God had never left her side. Tears began to fall from her eyes, and she whispered, "Yes, He is the one I've been looking for."

In that moment, she prayed her own prayer, asking for forgiveness and committing her life to the Father. The love of God broke through her pain, opening her heart to the healing and restoration she so desperately needed.

Scripture:

I will not leave you as orphans; I will come to you. – John 14:18 (NIV)

A Day of New Beginnings for Nepali Neighbors in Boston

Main Point: God brings the mission field to us, providing opportunities to share the Gospel with those who have never heard it.

Today was a life-changing day for 20 Nepali individuals, including a priest, who had never heard the name of Jesus or the story of His love. They are part of the 10,000 Nepali refugees who have relocated to Boston, struggling to adapt to a new life far from their Eastern roots. Unfortunately, the only outreach they had received up until now came from Mormons and Jehovah's Witnesses. But today, everything changed.

Doug and our team took them on a tour of Boston, sharing the city's Christian history and the legacy of its Christian founders. As we walked through the streets, the history of our city came alive, and our new friends began to ask questions, their hearts full of wonder.

Nick, a YWAMer from Nepal, and his mother, who came to Christ through reading a tract, played a pivotal role in this outreach. Nick's mother had planted two churches in Nepal despite facing threats, and now, together with her son, they helped bridge the gap between these Nepali neighbors and the Gospel. As they shared the message of creation, redemption, and God's love, the group began to open their hearts.

For the first time, these Nepali individuals encountered the truth of Jesus Christ. They are now filled with questions and are beginning a journey of discovery. We are in awe of how God has brought them to our neighborhood, providing us with the opportunity to share the Gospel with them—something that is so difficult to do in their homeland.

This experience reminds me that the mission field isn't always far away—it's often right next door. Who is near to you that might need to

100

hear the love of Jesus? It really is about loving God and loving our neighbor as ourselves.

Scripture:

Go therefore and make disciples of all nations, baptizing them in the name of the Father and of the Son and of the Holy Spirit, teaching them to observe all that I have commanded you. – Matthew 28:19-20 (ESV)

Breaking Barriers in Elizabeth Prison: A Divine Opportunity

Main Point: God opens doors when we step out in faith, even when the path seems uncertain.

(Doug's Story) During my time in Elizabeth, New Jersey, I often passed by a towering 13-story prison, and I felt a burden in my heart to minister there. Though I had no connections or strategies, I prayed and believed that God would open a door for me to enter. One day, I felt God's prompting to simply make a phone call to the prison's chaplain. It seemed like the obvious thing to do, yet I had hesitated until that moment.

When I called, I was connected to a new chaplain, fresh in her position, who was incredibly open to our team coming in. She reached out to the warden, but he initially declined, citing restrictions on large groups. Yet, driven by a deep conviction, the chaplain told the warden that if he wanted her to keep the position, he would have to allow our team in. Astonishingly, the warden agreed, and just like that, we were granted access to the prison.

This led to years of fruitful ministry in Elizabeth's prison, where we ministered to both youth and women. I recall one time when the women seemed so hardened, but as we performed a drama about the Gospel, their faces softened, and many came forward to accept Jesus.

During that time, I also introduced them to the Holy Spirit, and when I prayed for one woman to be filled, something miraculous happened— her sneakers, which were defective and hadn't lit up, suddenly glowed as I laid hands on her. This miracle was witnessed by the guards, and their hearts began to soften as well.

The prison became more open to our ministry, and over time, we saw countless lives transformed. We had the incredible privilege of sharing the Gospel in places we had once only dreamed of, all because we stepped out in faith, trusting that God would make a way.

Scripture:

But Jesus looked at them and said, "With man this is impossible, but with God all things are possible." – Matthew 19:26 (ESV)

Proclaiming the Gospel in the Heart of Israel: A Mission of Courage and Faith

Main Point: God's power opens doors even in the most hostile environments, and faith in Him brings transformation and boldness in sharing the Gospel.

(Doug's Story) During a mission trip to Israel, our team set out with the goal of sharing the Gospel with the Jewish people, despite being told that the Jews were uninterested and that success would be minimal.

We persevered, preaching daily, and saw many come to Christ. The breakthrough came on Christmas Eve when we learned that Bethlehem would be open to visitors, despite being controlled by hostile forces. With the world watching, we saw it as an opportunity to proclaim the Gospel in the heart of this historic city.

As we arrived, I struck up a conversation with a man sitting next to me on the bus who turned out to be a missionary from Sudan. Despite the danger, he agreed to translate for us in Arabic.

We went to Manger Square, set up our sound system, and began our performance. As we acted out the Gospel story, a crowd of over 600 men gathered, and tensions rose. Suddenly, a group of Arabic soldiers arrived, and we feared for our safety. But to our astonishment, the leader of the soldiers intervened, asking the crowd to give us space to continue our performance, offering us protection.

The crowd became more receptive, and at the end of the drama, I gave an altar call for salvation. Hundreds of men raised their hands to accept

Christ. Afterward, the missionary handed out over 600 Arabic Bibles, and to our surprise, none of the men rejected them. They hid them carefully, knowing they had received something precious.

God had used our time there to soften hearts and bring His peace to a tumultuous region.

Our mission continued in Tel Aviv, where we faced opposition from a hostile group trying to stop our outreach. But, as we stood firm, the people of the area rallied behind us, and even a store owner came out to support us, offering us cake and chocolate as a thank you for our courage. We continued to share the Gospel, seeing many come to Christ, including several Russian Muslims who accepted Jesus after witnessing our boldness.

In Jerusalem, we faced one final challenge as we performed for a hostile crowd. A Jewish man tried to shut us down, but a Jewish woman intervened, standing up to him so we could continue our show. We also had the chance to challenge two rabbis about the nature of salvation, leading to a powerful conversation on grace versus good works.

This mission in Israel—across Bethlehem, Tel Aviv, and Jerusalem—was one of the most dangerous yet fruitful experiences of our lives. We saw countless lives transformed, both Jewish and Arab, and God's protection was evident every step of the way.

During these six weeks, we saw over 150 people come to Christ, far exceeding the expected outcome. Our boldness and faith in Him led to incredible breakthroughs, proving that when God calls us to step out in faith, He will make a way.

Scripture:

For I am not ashamed of the gospel, because it is the power of God that brings salvation to everyone who believes. – Romans 1:16 (NIV)

Stand for Integrity in Athens

Main Point: Following Christ means embracing integrity, even when the cost seems high, and trusting God to provide.

(Doug's Story) Our journey in Athens began with a simple but profound mission—sharing the Gospel with those who needed it most. After weeks of travel, our team from the School of Evangelism arrived at Camping Varkeza, and I was confronted with my own personal struggle. Leaving our home in Western Pennsylvania, where our family had deep roots, was a difficult transition.

The comfort of familiar places and people was replaced by a life of uncertainty, where everything was different, including our living arrangements and the limited resources we had.

Doug and I made do, creating a simple life with a small tent, a table built from broken crates, and walks along the Mediterranean with our daughters, Rachel and Bethany. It was a humbling experience that forced me to confront my identity, not as someone recognized for success, but as a child of God, stripped of worldly comforts.

Meanwhile, Doug joined the outreach team in Piraeus, a seaport area in Athens where many foreign sailors, stranded after their contracts ended, were waiting for work. Doug and the team began to share the Gospel with these sailors, many of whom came from African nations. As they spent time together, the sailors opened up, but they also revealed a deeply compromised lifestyle, resorting to bribery just to survive.

Doug, with great courage, confronted them, explaining that following Christ meant obedience and trust in God—not relying on their own means.

For days, the team waited in silence as the sailors walked away, rejecting the call to live honestly. It felt like a defeat. But then, one day, a sailor stood up and proclaimed, "I have tar on my clothes from where I slept on the dock last night. I will no longer lie or pay a bribe. I have decided to follow Jesus."

His bold declaration was met with shock, but it was also an invitation for others to follow his example. The next day, as he went for a job interview, the interviewers asked him the familiar question: "How much do you want this job? What are you willing to give to secure it?" With faith and quiet courage, he responded, "I have decided to follow Jesus, and I cannot pay a bribe for this job."

What happened next was nothing short of miraculous. In a twist of grace, the interviewer, impressed by his honesty, hired him without the bribe, a moment of divine provision. This breakthrough was a turning point, and soon after, other sailors began to return, embracing the truth of Christ, realizing that following Jesus meant living a life of integrity, even in the face of difficulty.

Doug's decision to stand firm, and the sailor's courageous act of faith, demonstrated that the cost of discipleship is high, but the rewards of trust and obedience to God are immeasurable. This moment in Athens marked a profound shift, where the Gospel became not just words, but a living reality that transformed lives and deepened the faith of all involved.

Scripture:

"But the one who stands firm to the end will be saved." – Matthew 24:13 (NIV)

The Power of Timing in Sharing the Gospel

Main Point: God can use any method to open hearts to His love, and sometimes the most unexpected moments lead to powerful transformations.

While on a summer outreach in Poland, our team prepared to do a street drama to share the Gospel with the local community. We met Becky, a YWAMer who had been in Poland for a year. When I told her our plans for street mime and sharing the Gospel, she was shocked. "You can't do that here," she said. "You need to build relationships first, and only then can you share the Gospel. This kind of street ministry won't work."

I was surprised by her comment, as our team had been doing similar ministry in other Polish cities, and hundreds of people had responded to the Gospel. Still, I invited her to join us and watch. Becky hesitated but stayed, possibly unsure of being associated with our approach.

At the end of the drama, when we gave the invitation, many in the crowd prayed aloud, committing their lives to Jesus. As we usually did, our team gathered around those who had prayed to share the Gospel more deeply, using the wordless book. Becky joined one of the small groups, and, to her surprise, many people prayed with tears, sincerely accepting Jesus.

Afterward, Becky approached me, deeply moved. "I've been here for nine months, building relationships, waiting for the right moment to share. But today, in just a few hours, I've seen so many people open their hearts to Jesus. I feel like I've missed so many opportunities, and now my time is almost up."

We prayed for God to open more opportunities for Becky in her remaining time. A few days later, I received an email from her: "Do you remember me? The YWAMer from Nowy Sącz? After our talk, I went home and met with Mary, a friend I had been spending time with. I asked her if she wanted to hear the Gospel. She said yes, and I prayed with her to receive Jesus. It was such a joyful moment."

Becky shared how she had learned a powerful lesson: while relationships are important, God can open doors for us to share His love at any time. She had always avoided street evangelism before but now saw its effectiveness. "Lord, please use me in my last 13 days here," she prayed. "I see now how important it is to always be looking for opportunities to share Your love."

Through this experience, Becky discovered that the Holy Spirit works in His timing, and even in the most unexpected moments, hearts can be opened to the message of salvation.

Scripture:

"And how can they hear without someone preaching to them? And how can anyone preach unless they are sent?" As it is written, "How beautiful are the feet of those who bring good news!" – Romans 10:14-15 (NIV)

Finding the Key: Cultural Sensitivity and the Power of Honor

Main Point: Understanding and respecting cultural values can open doors for sharing the Gospel in unexpected ways.

(Doug's Story) In 1987, we took a team to Taiwan with high hopes of sharing the Gospel, despite being warned that it could take up to seven years to see a single conversion. This statement, made by seasoned missionaries, could have easily discouraged us, but we were determined to see fruit from our two-week trip.

We had prepared ourselves to engage with the Taiwanese people, and we believed that God would provide opportunities for us to share His love.

Upon arriving, we were quickly introduced to an outreach house near the factory section of town, where we engaged with workers who came for food and fellowship. One evening, Miss Nan, a tiny woman approached me, and through an interpreter, we began discussing Jesus. She expressed interest but, when asked if she understood what it meant to follow Jesus, her face turned serious and fearful.

"I could never trust Jesus," she said. "I am terrified of the Buddhas. They would bring disaster into my life." After that, she ended the conversation, leaving us with a sense of defeat. This was the kind of moment we had been warned about—the kind that takes years to break through.

Our team discussed what had happened, realizing most of our efforts had ended with closed doors. But instead of giving up, we prayed for God to show us a way forward. The next day, we decided to perform our "DOORS" drama in a local park.

Hundreds gathered to watch, but as soon as Doug spoke, the crowd fled. We moved to another spot, and the same thing happened—another large crowd, and then they dispersed before we could speak.

As discouragement set in, Doug had an idea. Looking at Steve Braun, our guest preacher, he said, "In this culture, there is a deep respect for elders. What if we adopt Steve as our elder and ask the crowd to listen to him out of respect for his age?" Steve, although not an elderly man, agreed to play along. We introduced him as "Father Steve" and made a special announcement to the crowd, asking them to honor him and listen to his words after the performance.

This time, the crowd stayed, captivated by the drama. As soon as it ended, Steve shared the Gospel, and many people responded. It was a breakthrough moment that came from understanding the cultural value of honoring elders—a key that unlocked the hearts of the Taiwanese people.

Miss Nan also met us again on one of our morning outreaches to the park, and this time she listened and received Jesus, convinced that He would protect her and be with her on her new journey of faith.

Pastor Steve would go on to return to Taiwan several times, planting churches and continuing the work that began with a small act of cultural respect. This experience reminded us that with the Holy Spirit's guidance, there is always a door to open, even when it seems impossible. We just need to listen, pray, and be open to God's creative ways of reaching people.

Scripture:

For though I am free from all, I have made myself a servant to all, that I might win more of them. – 1 Corinthians 9:19 (ESV)

The Power of a Seed: A Teacher's Impact in the Classroom

Main Point: The Holy Spirit can work powerfully in the hearts of students, even when we don't explicitly invite them to Jesus.

I was offered a third-grade teaching position at a Christian Academy, and during the interview, I was informed that I was not allowed to give a salvation invitation to the students. The school had experienced situations where students felt pressured to accept Christ, and they wanted to avoid that.

This was a first for me—a Christian school asking me not to directly invite students to receive Jesus. Despite this, I felt certain the position was from the Lord, so I accepted and trusted God had a plan.

Throughout the first few weeks, I talked about Jesus in subtle ways—sharing parts of my testimony, explaining how God is our creator, and mentioning how faith has shaped the lives of great historical figures.

At the end of each day, we took time to write down homework. One day, I noticed a girl taking extra time with her homework pad. When I walked past, I saw she had written "Get saved tonight!" with a big star next to it. My heart prayed quietly, "Lord, hear her heart."

The next morning, she entered the class with more excitement than usual. As we checked homework, she handed me her pad, and there was a huge checkmark next to "Get saved tonight." I smiled and said, "I'm praying for you and your faith in Jesus. He has heard your heart."

A few days later, during sharing time, she gave a testimony of praying to receive the Lord. One by one, my students shared that they, too, had accepted Jesus into their hearts. I never directly invited them, but the Holy Spirit had worked in their hearts. I realized that my role as their teacher was to be a witness of God's love, and the Holy Spirit did the rest.

Scripture:

One who plants and one who waters are one in purpose, and each will be rewarded according to their labor. – 1 Corinthians 3:8 (NIV)

"The Lamb Has Won": A Victory for Freedom and Faith in Timisoara

Main Point: True courage is stepping out in faith, even when facing fear, trusting that God will provide the right opportunities and protection for His mission.

On December 16, 1989, the Romanian people took to the streets of Timisoara to resist the brutal communist regime of Nicolae Ceaușescu. For 42 years, Ceaușescu had oppressed the nation through military force, rationing food and building mansions while his people starved.

The protests were met with violent retaliation; children and mothers were killed in the streets. But despite the violence, the soldiers—who were also Romanian—refused to fire on their own people.

Victory Square, where many lives were lost, became a sacred place, symbolizing the people's desire for freedom and justice. Amid the chaos, secret disciples of Jesus had written messages in their windows that read, "The Lamb has won." This became a rallying cry for the people of Romania, and eventually, Ceaușescu's regime would fall.

In 1991, Doug traveled to Timisoara with a team, moved by the social needs of the country. The nation was free, but there was still a deep sense of hopelessness. One of their key objectives was to reach the people of Timisoara with the Gospel.

Doug's team performed the DOORS drama in Victory Square, where a woman named Dr. Elizabeth, the director of the Timisoara Pediatric Hospital, had a life-changing encounter with Jesus.

Years later, Doug returned with a youth team from the Joshua Generation. The situation had changed—though Romania was now free, the government had begun cracking down on public gatherings. Despite the warnings from local believers, Doug felt called to share the Gospel in the very place where the revolution had begun. Victory Square, where many had sacrificed their lives for freedom, was also the place where freedom in Christ needed to be proclaimed.

With caution, Doug and his team set up in the Square, but as they began their performance, the police moved in and demanded they cease immediately. At that moment, a Romanian man who had greeted the team earlier stepped forward. He was the director of the human rights division of the city—someone who had spent years in prison for his faith under the communist regime. He had sensed God's leading that morning to walk through Victory Square, and when he saw the YWAM team, he knew his mission: to help them share the Gospel.

He presented his official seal to the police, and within moments, the officers dispersed. The crowd that had gathered listened as Doug invited them to receive Christ. Over 100 people knelt in the street, praying to accept Jesus as their Savior. The director, who had been led by God to intervene, smiled with approval, knowing the victory was not just political but spiritual.

As Doug reflected on the day's events, he realized that the Lamb had indeed won—not just in the hearts of the people of Timisoara but in the hearts of those who were willing to step out in faith. Courage isn't the absence of fear; it's trusting God and moving forward despite it, knowing that He will provide the opportunities and the protection needed to fulfill His will.

Scripture:

For God gave us a spirit not of fear but of power and love and self-control. – 2 Timothy 1:7 (ESV)

————

Our Message

What exactly are we sharing when we share our faith? At the center of all evangelism is the Gospel—the good news of Jesus Christ. But sometimes, we assume people already know it. This section brings us back to the simplicity and power of the message that changes lives.

These chapters will help you clearly present who Jesus is, why He came, and how He invites people into a relationship with God. You don't need to preach a sermon—you just need to share the truth with love, clarity, and confidence. The Gospel is still good news—and you've been entrusted with it.

Section Five
Every Way

Chapter 27
Open Doors – God Makes a Way

I pray that now at last by God's will the way may be opened for me to come to you. – Romans 1:10 (NIV)

Because a great door for effective work has opened to me, and there are many who oppose me. – 1 Corinthians 16:9 (NIV)

Now when I went to Troas to preach the gospel of Christ and found that the Lord had opened a door for me. – 2 Corinthians 2:12 (NIV)

What he opens no one can shut, and what he shuts no one can open... See, I have placed before you an open door that no one can shut. – Revelation 3:7–8 (NIV)

"God opens doors no man can shut. Walk through them in faith."

––––––

The doors are there. The harvest is ready. Be bold and walk through.

God is opening doors. Will you walk through them?

People Are Not Too Hard – The Harvest Is Ready

We have heard the same discouraging phrase on every continent: "You just don't understand how things are here. These people are harder than other places—they don't want to hear about Jesus." Local believers, often weary from trying, speak these words with disappointment. But discouragement can cloud the vision Jesus gave us: "The harvest is plentiful."

113

While it's true that some areas seem spiritually resistant, we've discovered time and again that God opens doors—sometimes unexpectedly, sometimes miraculously. And when He opens a door, no one can shut it.

Liberia: Representing the King

During Liberia's civil war in the 1990s, we brought relief supplies with Faith Christian Center. We were invited to a reception hosted by the U.S. ambassador. Plates were golden. The setting, royal. When the ambassador arrived, we stood in awe.

In that moment, I sensed God say, "You are My ambassador. He represents a country—but you represent My Kingdom." It was humbling and clarifying. I thought of my small compromises, my occasional anger. But as an ambassador of Christ, my life now reflected Him. That realization changed how I lived every day.

Greece: Integrity in the Midst of Desperation

In Athens, our YWAM team ministered to African sailors stranded in Pirarus. Legally barred from employment due to Greek hiring laws, they survived through bribes and deceit.

When we shared that trusting Jesus meant turning from lies and bribery, the bus emptied. But a few days later, one sailor returned. "I have decided to follow Jesus," he declared. He had slept on the dock rather than lie about housing. He refused to pay a bribe.

Days later, he was hired without a bribe. The official said, "We need honest workers like you." His testimony transformed others. One by one, the men chose Jesus—and jobs came without corruption. The Gospel spread. A new church was born—on that very bus.

Goffstown, New Hampshire: The Long Game

When our sons joined little league, we chose not to allow them to play Sunday games. At first, we were excluded by other parents. But when a teammate, Meagan, was diagnosed with cancer, we helped organize a community fundraiser.

At opening day, Doug asked to pray for Meagan publicly. With 600 players, parents, and officials bowing their heads, it became one of the holiest moments in our town. Later, Meagan recovered—and months later, gave her life to Jesus at a youth outreach.

What began with boundary-setting ended with hearts opened. Many who once kept their distance now saw Jesus through our family.

Brazil: Faith Over Fear

In 1974, we were newlyweds when invited to join a missions trip to Brazil. Obstacles mounted: no money, a pregnancy, a doctor's refusal to sign medical forms. But we prayed. Doug sold his treasured 1947 Plymouth Coupe to raise funds.

In Brazil, over 700 people came to Christ. The sacrifice was worth it. Our faith grew. The Gospel moved. And that car? Its value couldn't compare with eternal fruit.

Conclusion: The Holy Spirit Opens the Way

There is no single method. There is only faithful obedience. Whether through street drama, personal conversations, mercy ministries, or bold preaching—God opens doors.

Your role is to pray, listen, and step through the doors He opens. Sometimes it takes time. Sometimes it takes cultural understanding. Sometimes it takes tears and sacrifice. But every time, it takes the Holy Spirit.

Be available. Be courageous. Be a messenger.

Lessons Learned

Discouragement often clouds our vision, acting like a smokescreen that hides what God is already doing behind the scenes. Even when we can't see it, He is preparing hearts to receive the truth. In moments where it feels like doors are closed, cultural sensitivity and Spirit-led discernment can make all the difference—unlocking opportunities that once felt out of reach. Obedience to God's call may require sacrifice, but it always leads to fruit. There is no single formula for sharing the Gospel. Instead, we are called to use the open doors God provides, walking through them with faith. Often, your life, your story, and your compassion are the very first chapters in someone else's journey toward salvation.

Application

Walking Through the Door

- Start each day by asking God for divine appointments.
- Look beyond appearances—people who seem closed may be the most ready.
- Don't let fear or cultural barriers keep you from sharing.
- Partner with others to learn, adapt, and grow in evangelism.
- Step through the door God opens, even when it feels uncomfortable.

Reflection & Discussion Questions

1. Have you ever encountered what seemed like a closed door in evangelism? What happened?

2. Which of these stories spoke most deeply to you? Why?

3. What cultural or relational "key" might God use through you?

4. Are you praying for God to open doors in your life and community?

5. How can you be more sensitive to divine appointments each day?

Chapter 28
All Ways – Every Means Possible

But what does it matter? The important thing is that in every way, whether from false motives or true, Christ is preached. And because of this I rejoice. – Philippians 1:18 (NIV)

But you will receive power when the Holy Spirit comes on you; and you will be my witnesses in Jerusalem, and in all Judea and Samaria, and to the ends of the earth. – Acts 1:8 (NIV)

So the message about the Lord spread widely and had a powerful effect. – Acts 19:20 (NLT)

"God uses all kinds of methods to reach all kinds of people. There is no one-size-fits-all Gospel delivery system."

———

You don't have to be like someone else. You just have to be available. The Holy Spirit will use all ways to draw people to Jesus.

Every Way Possible

One day, I sat down with my Bible, a pen, and a question: What is the right way to communicate Christ to this generation? I began reading the book of Acts—and what I found changed everything.

The early church didn't craft a marketing strategy or a perfect technique. They simply lived the Gospel. They adapted to their surroundings and seized every opportunity. Their methods varied: house-to-house fellowship, miracles, public preaching, one-on-one conversations, martyrdom, and even accidental divine appointments.

They didn't ask, "Which way is best?" Instead, they pursued all ways.

So must we.

The Gospel is still the power of God for salvation. And the human heart still longs for love, identity, forgiveness, healing, purpose, and peace. Across cultures and centuries, people have needed what only Jesus can give. Technology and society may change, but soul needs remain.

I remember an email from a young woman in Poland who had encountered our team. She was touched not by our flawless strategy, but by the honesty and love of the team members. "I saw something real in your group," she wrote, "and I want to know more."

Lessons Learned

The book of Acts reveals that God works in many ways:

- **Personal Connections** – Philip and the Ethiopian (Acts 8)
- **The Power of the Spirit** – Empowerment and boldness (Acts 1:8)
- **Strategic Community** – Ongoing fellowship (Acts 2:42–47)
- **Mass Evangelism** – Peter preaching to 3,000 (Acts 2:12–41)
- **Healing and Miracles** – Peter and John with the crippled man (Acts 3:1–4:4)
- **Influence in High Places** – Priests believing (Acts 6:7)
- **Missionary Journeys** – Churches strengthened (Acts 16)
- **Apologetics** – Paul at the Areopagus (Acts 17)
- **Workplace Ministry** – Paul, Aquila, and Priscilla (Acts 18)
- **House Gatherings** – Lydia's home and others (Acts 16:13–15)
- **Divine Appointments** – Cornelius and Peter (Acts 10)
- **Everyday Faithfulness** – Daily teaching and proclamation (Acts 5:42)

Application

Every Way Matters

Do you host meals and share stories? That's an opportunity for evangelism.

Do you pray with strangers? That's an opportunity for evangelism.

Do you share devotionals online? That's an opportunity for evangelism.

Do you meet practical needs with compassion? That's an opportunity for evangelism.

All these ways are valid if Jesus is lifted up. These acts of generous kindness open the door for a conversation about the Gospel. They shouldn't be the end, but the beginning that makes an opportunity for Salvation.

Let's stop competing over the best method and instead rejoice that Christ is preached.

Remember: the method is flexible. The message is not. And the motive? It must always be love.

Reflection & Discussion Questions

1. How has God uniquely gifted you to share the Gospel?

2. Which method of evangelism feels most natural to you?

3. Have you ever judged someone else's method of outreach? Why?

4. How can you support other believers in their unique calling to evangelize?

5. What opportunities in your daily life can be used to point others to Jesus?

Chapter 29
The Father's Heart for the Lost

Guest Contributor: Christine St. Cyr

For the Son of Man came to seek and to save the lost. – Luke 19:10 (NIV)

"Break my heart for what breaks Yours." – *A prayer that changes everything*

A Personal Journey Toward God's Heart (by Christine St. Cyr)

I never thought of myself as an evangelist. I wasn't the one preaching on the street corner or hosting big crusades. But somewhere deep inside me, there was always this longing—a quiet, persistent desire to share my faith with people who didn't know Him. It wasn't something I manufactured. It grew over time, planted by the love of Jesus and watered by experiences that changed me forever.

The First Marker: A Dream That Broke Me

When I was still a young Christian, I had a dream. I can't say for sure it was from God, but it felt significant. In the dream, I entered Heaven. The joy was overwhelming as I ran into the Lord's arms. We embraced warmly, and my heart was filled with love. But then, over His shoulder, I noticed a group of people standing far off in a shadowed corner. They stood silently, waiting. "Who are they?" I asked the Lord. He looked at me with pure love and said, "Those are the people I placed in your life—and you didn't tell them about Me. "There was no anger in His voice. No shame. Only deep, sorrowful love. As I opened my mouth to ask, "Are they lost?"—I woke up. The emotions that flooded me were intense:

sorrow, regret—but above all else, overwhelming love. A love too big to keep to myself. From that day forward, I knew: I could not stay silent.

The Second Marker: A Prayer God Answered Immediately

At one point, desperate to love more deeply, I prayed, "Lord, break my heart for what breaks Yours."

I had no idea how quickly He would respond. The very next day, my 16-year-old stepson—angry, hurting—left our home. He no longer wanted anything to do with our Christian life. He walked out the door and into a lifestyle of rebellion, and my heart shattered into pieces. I would cry silently at night, sneaking downstairs so my husband wouldn't hear the sobs wracking my body. In my grief, God whispered: "This is how I feel for every lost child. "He wasn't punishing me. He was letting me feel His heart—a heart broken over every prodigal wandering far from home.

The Third Marker: A New Understanding of the Prodigal Son

At our School of Evangelism, missionary Nick Savoca shared a powerful perspective: "What if the older brother had gone after the prodigal? What if, seeing his father's grief, he had said, "I'll find him. I'll tell him he's loved and bring him home. "'That image changed me. We are not just meant to stay safely at home while others are lost. We are called to go—because we love the Father, and because we love them.

Lessons Learned

I learned that sharing the Gospel isn't about strategy or obligation—it's about carrying the very heartbeat of God into the world. It's about allowing His compassion to overtake your own comfort. It's about seeing people not as strangers, but as beloved sons and daughters who just need to hear: Come home.

Over time, God showed me that love must be stronger than fear, stronger than awkwardness, stronger than rejection. There are moments when you will be compelled to speak—where no excuse will quiet the burning inside you. There are moments when you'll find yourself standing in a McDonald's, watching a woman behind the counter, and knowing that

God wants you to speak a word of encouragement—whether or not it makes sense. And when you say yes, when you cross the line from silence to love, you'll see tears fall, walls crumble, hearts awaken. You'll see God move. You won't regret it.

Application

Let Love Move You

God doesn't force us to love people. He invites us to share His heart. He longs for us to feel what He feels—to be so gripped by compassion that we must go to the hurting, the addicted, the lonely, and the broken. He calls us into grocery stores, into schools, into workplaces, into broken neighborhoods—not because we are saviors, but because He wants His love to be visible through us. He doesn't want a silent Church. He wants a singing, weeping, rejoicing army—people who know His love so deeply that they cannot hold it back.

If you yield to Him—if you say yes—He will fill you with His heart. And in doing so, He will send you to places where you will be His hands, His voice, His embrace to the lost. He will send you to be part of someone else's miracle.

Discussion Questions

1. Have you ever experienced a moment where you knew you should share your faith, but hesitated? What held you back?
2. How does the idea of the older brother going after the prodigal change your view of evangelism?
3. What emotions do you feel when you consider the reality of eternal separation from God? How can that awareness change your daily life?
4. In what areas of your community (schools, workplaces, neighborhoods) do you sense God calling you to "go"?
5. What steps can you take to let love—not fear—be the driving force in sharing your faith?

About the Author

Christine St. Cyr is a passionate follower of Jesus Christ whose greatest desire is to see hearts transformed by the love of God. She speaks and writes about living a life fully yielded to God's call to share the Gospel, drawing from her personal journey of brokenness, compassion, and relentless hope.

Conclusion

When God Opens the Door

What does it look like to live a life that says "yes" to God? It looks like ordinary believers becoming bold messengers. It looks like open hearts meeting open hands.

It looks like obedience in motion—walking through doors God opens.

Throughout this book, you've read real stories—raw, honest, and hope-filled—of people just like you. People who didn't have all the answers but chose to trust the One who does. You've seen how fear can be overcome, how apathy can be shaken, and how the Gospel still has the power to change lives.

Evangelism is not reserved for the extroverted, the seminary-trained, or the fearless. It's for the willing. The ones who will walk across a room, or a street, or a city to share the message of Jesus. It's for those who know they aren't perfect—but believe that the grace of God is.

There are open doors everywhere.

- A coworker grieving silently.
- A neighbor facing uncertainty.
- A student wrestling with identity.
- A stranger who wonders if anyone cares.

Behind every door is a heart. And behind every heart is a story. You may be the one God sends to step into that story.

Jesus didn't say "Stay." He said, "Go." He didn't say "Convince." He said, "Be My witness." He didn't say "Figure it all out." He said, "Follow Me."

Now the baton is in your hand. The stories you've read are not the end— they are an invitation. God is writing new chapters through you.

Will you walk through the door?

Let's go.

————

Every Way

God uses all kinds of people in all kinds of places. Whether it's across the world or across the table, there are doors opening all around us. This final section is about being ready—for any moment, any method, and any opportunity God brings your way.

Evangelism isn't just for street corners or special events. It's for kitchens and coffee shops, classrooms and commutes. However, He leads you, just be available. These chapters will inspire you to walk through every open door, trusting that when you show up, God will too.

About the Author

Debra Tunney is a missionary, educator, speaker, and author with a lifelong passion for helping ordinary believers step into the extraordinary plans God has for them. For over five decades, she and her husband Doug have ministered across the globe—training teams, launching outreach initiatives, and equipping people to carry the hope of Jesus into their communities and beyond.

An experienced educator, Debra brings clarity, compassion, and practical insight to her teaching. She is a respected women's speaker and teaches Destiny by Design, a seminar that helps individuals discover their God-given calling and live with purpose. Whether leading city outreaches, mentoring young leaders, or teaching across cultures, Debra's message remains consistent: God is still opening doors—and He's calling you to walk through them.

She is also the author of A Legacy of Faith, a powerful collection of stories from her family's journey in missions, available in both English and Portuguese on Amazon and Barnes & Noble.

Debra and Doug make their home in Philadelphia, where they continue to mentor leaders and train and send teams into both local communities and nations around the world. They are the proud parents of four married adult children who carry their faith into diverse spheres—as educators, business leaders, professionals, and ministry leaders. With sixteen grandchildren, many of whom have already joined them on the mission field, their family is living out a vibrant, multigenerational legacy of faith, purpose, and service.